JUDITH SALLE'YONGUE, M.D., P.A.
PSYCHIATRIC MEDICINE
107-C COMMERCE STREET
GREENVILLE, NORTH CAROLINA 27834

PHONE (919) 355-2768

THE POWER TACTICS OF JESUS CHRIST
and other essays

by Jay Haley (as author, coauthor, editor)

Strategies of Psychotherapy

Family Therapy and Research: A Bibliography

*Advanced Techniques of Hypnosis and Therapy: Selected Papers of
Milton H. Erickson, M.D.*

Techniques of Family Therapy

Changing Families: A Family Therapy Reader

*Uncommon Therapy: The Psychiatric Techniques of Milton H.
Erickson, M.D.*

Problem Solving Therapy: New Strategies for Effective Family Therapy

Leaving Home

Reflections on Therapy, and Other Essays

Conversations with Milton H. Erickson, M.D.
   Volume 1: Changing Individuals
   Volume 2: Changing Couples
   Volume 3: Changing Children and Families

Jay Haley

▣▣ *THE POWER TACTICS*
▣▣ *OF JESUS CHRIST*

and other essays

Second Edition

THE TRIANGLE PRESS · Rockville, Md.

ISBN 0-931513-04-9

Manufactured in the United States of America
Library of Congress Catalog Card Number 86-50142.

Published by Triangle Press

Distributed by W. W. Norton & Co., Inc.
500 Fifth Avenue
New York, N. Y. 10110

W. W. Norton & Co., Ltd.
37 Great Russell Street
London, WC1B3NU

Contents

▣ Preface 1

▣ The Art of Psychoanalysis 5

▣ The Power Tactics of Jesus Christ 19

▣ The Art of Being a Schizophrenic 55

▣ The Art of Being a Failure as a Therapist 81

▣ In Defense of Psychoanalysis 89

▣ Towards a Rationalization for Directive
  Therapy 103

▣ How to Have an Awful Marriage 117

▣ Therapy — A New Phenomenon 137

Preface

Recently I was informed that a group of students wished to give a present to their professor on his retirement. Of all the gifts they might choose, a copy of THE POWER TACTICS OF JESUS CHRIST was the most valuable present they could offer. After searching the bookstores of the world, they had to give up. There was simply no copy to be found. To prevent such tragedies with elderly professors in the future, this new edition is being released. It has been brought up to date with two essays eliminated and four new ones added. The title essay remains, of course, as an appreciation of the skills of Jesus. What it takes to be a schizophrenic is still here, for readers interested in that career. Psychoanalysis is given a depth examination as an art, and the techniques required to fail as a therapist continue to be offered.

The new essays emphasize contemporary issues. For the participant in marriage — and we are all married, planning to be married, or avoiding that state — there is HOW TO HAVE AN AWFUL MARRIAGE. Looking back, psychoanalysis is given its place in history with IN DEFENSE OF PSYCHOANALYSIS. Looking forward in the world of changing people there is THERAPY — A NEW PHENOMENON and TOWARDS A RATIONALIZATION FOR DIRECTIVE THERAPY.

I wish to express acknowledgement of the publications in which three of the essays appeared. THE ART OF PSYCHO-ANALYSIS appeared in *ETC*, after being rejected by all the psychoanalysis journals. The ART OF BEING A FAILURE AS A THERAPIST appeared in the *Journal of Orthopsychiatry* and THE ART OF BEING SCHIZOPHRENIC appeared in *Voices*.

Jay Haley
Rockville, 1986

THE ART OF PSYCHOANALYSIS

Enough research has been done by social scientists to corroborate many of Freud's ideas about unconscious processes. Yet there has been surprisingly little scientific investigation of what actually occurs during psychoanalytic treatment. Fortunately this situation has been remedied by a scholar on the faculty of Potters College in Yeovil, England. Assigned a field trip in America, this anonymous student spent several years here studying the art of psychoanalysis both as a patient and a practitioner. His investigation culminated in a three-volume work entitled "*The Art of Psychoanalysis, or Some Aspects of a Structured Situation Consisting of Two-Group Interaction Which Embodies Certain of the Most Basic Principles of Oneupmanship.*" Like most studies written for Potters College the work was unpublished and accessible only to a few favored members of the clinical staff. However, a copy was briefly in this writer's hands, and he offers here a summary of the research findings for those who wish to foster the dynamic growth of Freudian theory and sharpen the techniques of a difficult art.

Unfamiliar terms will be translated into psychoanalytic terminology throughout this summary, but a few general definitions are necessary at once. First of all, a complete definition of the technical term "oneupmanship" would fill, and in fact has filled, a rather large encyclopedia. It can be defined briefly here as the art of putting a person "one-down." The term "one-down" is technically defined as that psychological state which exists in an individual who is not "one-up" on another person. To be "one-up" is technically defined as that psychological state of an individual who is not "one-down." To phrase these terms in popular language, at the risk of losing scientific rigor, it can be said that in any human relationship (and indeed among other mammals) one person is constantly maneuvering to imply that he is in a "superior position" to the other person in the relationship. This "superior position" does not necessarily mean superior in social status or economic position; many servants are masters at putting their employers one-down. Nor does it imply intellectual superiority as any intellectual knows who has been put "one-down" by a muscular garbage collector in a bout of Indian wrestling. "Superior position" is a relative term which is continually being defined and re-defined by the ongoing relationship. Maneuvers to achieve superior position may be crude or they may be infinitely subtle. For example, one is not usually in a superior position if he must ask another person for something. Yet he can ask for it in such a way that he is implying, "This is, of course, what I deserve." Since the number of ways of maneuvering oneself into a superior position are infinite, let us proceed at once to summarize the psychoanalytic techniques as described in the three volume study.

Psychoanalysis, according to Potter's study, is a dynamic psychological process involving two people, a patient and a psychoanalyst, during which the patient insists that the analyst be one-up while desperately trying to put him one-down, and the analyst insists that the patient remain one-down in order to help him learn to become one-up. The goal of the relationship is the amicable separation of analyst and patient.

Carefully designed, the psychoanalytic setting makes the superior position of the analyst almost invincible. First of all, the patient must voluntarily come to the analyst for help, thus conceding his inferior position at the beginning of the relationship. In addition, the patient accentuates his one-down position by paying the analyst money. Occasionally analysts have recklessly broken this structured situation by treating patients free of charge. Their position was difficult because the patient was not regularly reminded (on payday) that he must make a sacrifice to support the analyst, thus acknowledging the analyst's superior position before a word is said. It is really a wonder that any patient starting from this weak position could ever become one-up on an analyst, but in private discussions analysts will admit, and in fact tear at their hair while admitting, that patients can be extremely adroit and use such a variety of clever ploys* that an analyst must be nimble to maintain his superior position.

Space does not permit a review of the history of psychoanalysis here, but it should be noted that early in its development it became obvious that the analyst needed reinforcement of the setting if he was to remain one-up on patients more clever than he. An early reinforcement was the use of a couch for the patient to lie down upon. (This is often called "Freud's ploy," as are most ploys in psychoanalysis.) By placing the patient on a couch, the analyst gives the patient the feeling of having his feet up in the air and the knowledge that the analyst has both feet on the ground. Not only is the patient disconcerted by having to lie down while talking, but he finds himself literally below the analyst and so his one-down position is geographically emphasized. In addition, the analyst seats himself behind the couch where he can watch the patient but the patient cannot watch him. This gives the patient the sort of disconcerted feeling a person has when sparring with an opponent while blindfolded. Unable to see what response his ploys provoke, he is unsure when he is one-up and when one-down. Some patients try to solve this problem by saying something like, "I slept with my sister last night," and then whirling around to see how the analyst is responding. These "shocker" ploys usually fail in their effect. The analyst may twitch, but he has time to recover before the patient can whirl fully around and see him. Most analysts have developed ways of handling the whirling patient. As the patient turns, they are staring off into space, or doodling with a pencil, or braiding belts, or staring at tropical fish. It is essential that the rare patient who gets an opportunity to observe the analyst see only an impassive demeanor.

Another purpose is served by the position behind the couch. Inevitably what the analyst says becomes exaggerated in impor-

*A "ploy" is technically defined as a move or gambit which gives one an advantage in a relationship.

tance since the patient lacks any other means of determining his effect on the analyst. The patient finds himself hanging on the analyst's every word, and by definition he who hangs on another's words is one-down.

Perhaps the most powerful weapon in the analyst's arsenal is the use of silence. This falls in the category of "helpless" or "refuse to battle" ploys. It is impossible to win a contest with a helpless opponent since if you win you have won nothing. Each blow you strike is unreturned so that all you can feel is guilt for having struck while at the same time experiencing the uneasy suspicion that the helplessness is calculated. The result is suppressed fury and desperation — two emotions characterizing the one-down position. The problem posed for the patient is this: how can I get one up on a man who won't respond and compete with me for the superior position in fair and open encounter. Patients find solutions, of course, but it takes months, usually years, of intensive analysis before a patient finds ways to force a response from his analyst. Ordinarily the patient begins rather crudely by saying something like, "Sometimes I think you're an idiot." He waits for the analyst to react defensively, thus stepping one-down. Instead the analyst replies with the silence ploy. The patient goes further and says, "I'm *sure* you're an idiot." Still silence in reply. Desperately the patient says, "I said you were an idiot, damn you, and you are!" Again only silence. What can the patient do but apologize, thus stepping voluntarily into a one-down position. Often a patient discovers how effective the silence ploy is and attempts to use it himself. This ends when he realizes that he is paying a large sum each hour to lie silent on a couch. The psychoanalytic setting is calculatedly designed to prevent patients from using the ploys of analysts to attain equal footing (although as an important part of the cure the patient learns to use them effectively with other people).

Few improvements have been made on Freud's original brilliant design. As the basic plan for the hammer could not be improved upon by carpenters, so the use of the voluntary patient, hourly pay, the position behind the couch, and silence, are devices which have not been improved upon by practitioners of psycho-analysis.

Although the many ways of handling patients learned by the analyst cannot be listed here, a few general principles can be mentioned. Inevitably a patient entering analysis begins to use ploys which have put him one-up in previous relationships (this is called a "neurotic pattern"). The analyst learns to devastate these maneuvers of the patient. A simple way, for example, is to respond inappropriately to what the patient says. This puts the patient in doubt about everything he has learned in relationships with other people. The patient may say, "Everyone should be truthful," hoping to get the analyst to agree with him and thereby follow his lead. He who follows another's lead is one-down. The analyst may reply with silence, a rather weak ploy in this circumstance, or he may say, "Oh?" The "Oh?" is given just the proper inflection to imply, "How on earth could you have ever conceived such an idea?" This not only puts the patient in doubt about his statement, but in doubt about what the analyst means by "Oh?". Doubt is, of course, the first step toward one-downness. When in doubt the patient tends to lean on the analyst to resolve the doubt, and we lean on those who are superior to us. Analytic maneuvers designed to arouse doubt in a patient are instituted early in analysis. For example, the analyst may say, "I wonder if that's *really* what you're feeling." The use of "really" is standard in analytic practice. It implies the patient has motivations of which he is not aware. Anyone feels shaken, and therefore one-down, when this suspicion is put in his mind.

Doubt is related to the "unconscious ploy," an early development in psychoanalysis. This ploy is often considered the heart of analysis since it is the most effective way of making the patient unsure of himself. Early in an analysis the skilled analyst points out to the patient that he (the patient) has unconscious processes operating and is deluding himself if he thinks he really knows what he is saying. When the patient accepts this idea he can only rely on the analyst to tell him (or, as it is phrased, "to help him discover") what he really means. Thus he burrows himself deeper into the one-down position, making it easy for the analyst to top almost any ploy he devises. For example, the patient may cheer-fully describe what a fine time he had with his girl friend, hoping to arouse some jealousy (a one-down emotion) in the analyst. The appropriate reply for the analyst is, "I wonder what that girl *really* means to you." This raises a doubt in the patient whether he is having intercourse with a girl named Susy or an unconscious symbol. Inevitably he turns to the analyst to help him discover what the girl really means to him.

Regularly in the course of an analysis, particularly if the patient becomes obstreperous (uses resistance ploys), the analyst makes an issue of free association and dreams. Now a person must feel he knows what he is talking about to feel in a superior position. No one can maneuver to become one-up while free associating or narrating his dreams. The most absurd statements inevitably will be uttered. At the same time the analyst hints that there are meaningful ideas in this absurdity. This not only makes the patient feel that he is saying ridiculous things, but that he is saying things which the analyst sees meaning in and he doesn't. Such an experience would shake anyone, and inevitably drives the patient into a one-down position. Of course if the patient refuses to free associate or tell his dreams, the analyst reminds him that he is defeating himself by being resistant.

A resistance interpretation falls in the general class of "turning it back on the patient" ploys. All attempts, particularly successful ones, to put the analyst one-down can be interpreted as resistance to treatment. The patient is made to feel that it is *his* fault that therapy is going badly. Carefully preparing in advance, the skill-ful analyst informs the patient in the first interview that the path to happiness is difficult and he will at times resist getting well and indeed may even resent the analyst for helping him. With this background even a refusal to pay the fee or a threat to end the analysis can be turned into apologies with an impersonal attitude by the analyst (the "not taking it personally" ploy) and an interpretation about resistance. At times the analyst may let the patient re-enter the one-down position gently by pointing out that his resistance is a sign of progress and change taking place in him.

The main difficulty with most patients is their insistence on dealing directly with the analyst once they begin to feel some confidence. When the patient begins to look critically at the analyst and threaten an open encounter, several "distraction" ploys are brought into play. The most common is the "concentrate on the past" ploy. Should the patient discuss the peculiar way the analyst refuses to respond to him, the analyst will inquire, "I wonder if you've had this feeling before. Perhaps your parents weren't very responsive." Soon they are busy discussing the patient's childhood without the patient's ever discovering that the subject has been changed. Such a ploy is particularly effective when the patient begins to use what he has learned in analysis to make comments about the analyst.

In his training the young analyst learns the few rather simple rules that he must follow. The first is that it is essential to keep the patient feeling one-down while stirring him to struggle gamely in the hope that he can get one-up (this is called "transference"). Secondly, the analyst must never feel one-down (this is called "counter-transference"). The training analysis is designed to help the young analyst learn what it is like to experience a one-down position. By acting like a patient he learns what it feels like to conceive a clever ploy, deliver it expertly, and find himself put thoroughly one-down.

Even after seven or eight years in a training analysis seeing his weak ploys devastated, an analyst will occasionally use one with a patient and find himself forced into a one-down position. Despite the brilliant structure of the analytic fortress, and the arsenal of ploys learned in training, all men are human and to be human is to be occasionally one-down. The training emphasizes how to get out of the one-down position quickly when in it. The general ploy is to accept the one-down position "voluntarily" when it is inescapable. Finding the patient one-up, the analyst may say, "You have a point there," or "I must admit I made a mistake." The more daring analyst will say, "I wonder why I became a little anxious when you said that." Note that all these statements *seem* to show the analyst to be one-down and the patient one-up, but one-downness requires defensive behavior. By deliberately acknowledging his inferior position the analyst is actually maintaining his superior position, and the patient finds that once again a clever ploy has been topped by a helpless, or a refusal to do battle, ploy. At times the "acceptance" technique cannot be used because the analyst is too sensitive in that area. Should a patient discover that this analyst gets embarrassed when homosexual ideas are discussed, he may rapidly exploit this. The analyst who takes such comments personally is lost. His only chance for survival is to anticipate in his diagnostic interviews those patients capable of discovering and exploiting this weakness and refer them to analysts with different weaknesses.

The more desperate ploys by patients are also anticipated in analytic training. A patient will at times be so determined to get one-up on his analyst that he will adopt the "suicide" ploy. Many analysts immediately suffer a one-down feeling when a patient threatens suicide. They hallucinate newspaper headlines and hear their colleagues chuckling as they whisper the total number of patients who got one-up on them by jumping off the bridge. The common way to prevent the use of this ploy is to take it impersonally. The analyst says something like, "Well I'd be sorry if you blew your brains out, but I would carry on with my work." The patient abandons his plans as he realizes that even killing himself will not put him one-up on this man.

Orthodox psychoanalytic ploys can be highlighted by contrasting them with the more unorthodox maneuvers. There is, for example, the Rogerian system of ploys where the therapist merely repeats back what the patient says. This is an inevitably winning system. No one can top a person who merely repeats his ideas after him. When the patient accuses the therapist of being no use to him, the therapist replies, "You feel I'm no use to you." The patient says, "That's right, you're not worth a damn." The therapist says, "You feel I'm not worth a damn." This ploy, even more than the orthodox silence ploy, eliminates any triumphant feeling in the patient and makes him feel a little silly after awhile (a one-down feeling). Most orthodox analysts look upon the Rogerian ploys as not only weak but not quite respectable. They don't give the patient a fair chance.

The ethics of psychoanalysis require the patient be given at least a reasonably fair chance. Ploys which simply devastate the patient are looked down on. Analysts who use them are thought to need more analysis themselves to give them a range of more legitimate ploys and confidence in using them. For instance, it isn't considered proper to encourage a patient to discuss a subject and then lose interest when he does. This puts the patient one-down, but it is a wasted ploy since he wasn't trying to become one-up. If a patient makes such an attempt then of course losing interest may be a necessary gambit.

Another variation on orthodox psychoanalytic ploys demonstrates a few of their limitations. The psychotic continually demonstrates that he is superior to orthodox ploys. He refuses to "volunteer" for analysis. He won't take a sensible interest in money. He won't lie quietly on the couch and talk while the analyst listens out of sight behind him. The structure of the analytic situation seems to irritate the psychotic. In fact when orthodox ploys are used against him, the psychotic is likely to tear up the office and kick the analyst in the genitals (this is called an inability to establish a transference). The average analyst is made uncomfortable by psychotic ploys and therefore avoids such patients. Recently some daring therapists have found they can get one-up on a psychotic patient if they work in pairs. This is now called the "it takes two to put one down" therapy, or "multiple therapy." For example, if a psychotic talks compulsively and won't even pause to listen, two therapists enter the room and begin to converse with each other. Unable to restrain his curiosity (a one-down emotion) the psychotic will stop talking and listen, thus leaving himself open to be put one-down.

The master oneupman with psychotics is a controversial psychiatrist known affectionately in the profession as "The Bull." When a compulsive talker won't listen to him the Bull pulls a knife on the fellow and attracts his attention. No other therapist is so adroit at topping even the most determined patient. Other therapists require hospitals, attendants, shock treatments, lobotomies, drugs, restraints, and tubs, to place the patient in a sufficiently one-down position. The Bull, with mere words and the occasional flash of a pocket knife, manages to make the most difficult psychotic feel one-down.

An interesting contrast to the Bull is a woman known in the profession as "The Lovely Lady of the Lodge." Leading the league in subtle oneupmanship with psychotics, she avoids the Bull's ploys which are often considered rather crude and not always in the best of taste. If a patient insists he is God, the Bull will insist that *he* is God and force the patient to his knees, thus getting one-up in a rather straightforward way. To handle a similar claim by a patient, The Lady of the Lodge will smile and say, "All right, if you wish to be God, I'll let you." The patient is gently put one-down as he realizes that no one but God can *let* anyone else be God.

Although orthodox psychoanalytic ploys may be limited to work with neurotics no one can deny their success. The experienced analyst can put a patient one-down while planning where to have dinner at the same time. Of course this skill in oneupmanship has raised extraordinary problems when analysts compete with one another at meetings of the psychoanalytic associations. No other gathering of people exhibits so many complicated ways of gaining the upper hand. Most of the struggle at an analytic meeting takes place at a rather personal level, but the manifest content involves attempts to (1) demonstrate who was closest to Freud or can quote him most voluminously, and (2) who can confuse the most people by his daring extension of Freud's terminology. The man who can achieve both these goals best is generally elected president of the association.

The manipulation of language is the most startling phenomenon at an analytic meeting. Obscure terms are defined and redefined by even more obscure terms as analysts engage in furious theoretical discussions. This is particularly true when the point at issue is whether a certain treatment of a patient was *really* psychoanalysis or not. Such a point is inevitably raised when a particularly brilliant case history is presented.

What happens between analyst and patient, or the art of oneupmanship, is rarely discussed at the meeting (apparently the techniques are too secret for public discussion). This means the area for debate becomes the processes within the dark and dank interior of the patient. Attempting to outdo one another in explanations of the bizarre insides of patients, each speaker is constantly interrupted by shouts from the back of the hall such as, "Not at all! You're confusing an id impulse with a weak ego boundary!" or "Heaven help your patients if you call *that* cathexis!" Even the most alert analyst soon develops an oceanic feeling as he gets lost in flurries of energy theories, libidinal drives, instinctual forces, and super ego barriers. The analyst who can most thoroughly confuse the group leaves his colleagues feeling frustrated and envious (one-down emotions). The losers return to their studies to search their minds, dictionaries, science fiction journals, and Freud for even more elaborate metaphorical flights in preparation for the next meeting.

The ploys of analyst and patient can be summarized briefly as they occur during a typical course of treatment. Individual cases will vary depending on what maneuvers the individual patient uses (called "symptoms" by the analyst when they are ploys no sensible person would use), but a general trend is easy to follow. The patient enters analysis in the one-down posture by asking for help and promptly tries to put the therapist one-down by building him up. This is called the honeymoon of the analysis. The patient begins to compliment the therapist on how wonderful he is and how quickly he (the patient) expects to get well. The skilled analyst is not taken in by these maneuvers (known as the "Reichian resistance" ploys). When the patient finds himself continually put one-down, he changes tactics. He becomes mean, insulting, threatens to quit analysis, and casts doubt upon the sanity of the analyst. These are the "attempts to get a human response" ploys. They meet an impassive, impersonal wall as the

analyst remains silent or handles the insults with a simple statement like, "Have you noticed this is the second Tuesday afternoon
you've made such a comment? I wonder what there is about
Tuesday," or "You seem to be reacting to me as if I'm someone
else." Frustrated in his aggressive behavior (resistance ploys), the
patient capitulates and ostensibly hands control of the situation
back to the analyst. Again building the analyst up, he leans on
him, hangs on his every word, insists how helpless he is and how
strong the analyst, and waits for the moment when he will lead
the analyst along far enough to devastate him with a clever ploy.
The skilled analyst handles this nicely with a series of "condescending" ploys, pointing out that the patient must help himself
and not expect anyone to solve everything for him. Furious, the
patient again switches from subservient ploys to defiant ploys.
By this time he has learned techniques from the analyst and is
getting better. He uses what insight (ploys unknown to laymen)
he has gained to try in every way to define the relationship as
one in which the analyst is one-down. This is the difficult period
of the analysis. However, having carefully prepared the ground
by a thorough diagnosis (listing weak points) and having instilled
a succession of doubts in the patient about himself, the analyst
succeeds in topping the patient again and again as the years pass.
Ultimately a remarkable thing happens. The patient rather casually tries to get one-up, the analyst puts him one-down, and the
patient does not become disturbed by this. He has reached a point
where he doesn't *really* care whether the analyst is in control of
the relationship or whether he is in control. In other words, he
is cured. The analyst then dismisses him, timing this maneuver
just before the patient is ready to announce that he is leaving.
Turning to his waiting list, the analyst invites in another patient
who, by definition, is someone compelled to struggle to be one-
up and disturbed if he is put one-down. And so goes the day's
work in the difficult art of psychoanalysis.

THE POWER TACTICS
OF JESUS CHRIST

Now that Christianity has declined as a force in the world of ideas, we are free to appreciate the skills of Jesus Christ. The innovations of Jesus as an organizer and a leader of men have been overlooked by most Christians and social scientists. Typically the credit for his achievements has been given to the Lord, which seems unfair, or to later followers like Paul, which seems even more unfair. When one abandons the idea that it was the intervention of a God or later leaders which led to the success of Jesus, his ability as an organizer appears incredible. This single individual designed the strategy of an organization which not only took over the Roman Empire but ultimately held absolute power over the populace of the western world for many hundreds of years. No other person has approached such an accomplishment. Until the leaders of communist and other mass movements appeared in this century there was not even a contender.

To understand the messianic revolutionists of today one must appreciate the legacy left by Jesus. Men such as Lenin and Trotsky in Russia, Hitler in Germany, Mussolini in Italy, Mao Tse-Tung and Ho Chi Minh in Asia, Castro in Cuba and black power leaders like Elijah Mohammed in the United States all discredit Jesus in their public statements — the organization he founded is still influential in the establishments to be overthrown. Yet their debt to him is far greater than they would acknowledge. The most obvious debt such leaders owe Jesus is his basic innovation: the idea of striking for power by organizing the poor and the powerless. For centuries this idea of Jesus was overlooked and so the poor were not a threat to the establishment; the most that could be expected of them was an occasional sporadic riot. In this century the poor must be taken into account everywhere because there are men who will devote their lives to rousing and organizing them. The ideology of contemporary mass movement leaders differs in certain ways from that of Jesus, but it will be argued here that their basic strategy did not arise spontaneously in our time but was outlined in the New Testament and designed in Galilee by one man.

Since all we know of Jesus is based upon the writings of members of his organization, questions about his contribution can always be raised because of doubts about the objectivity and authenticity of the Bible. The view offered here will take the gospel writers at their word; they were describing a man who formed and led a movement. In regard to the text, the position taken is fundamentalist with a bias in favor of the Synoptic gospels. Many generations of men, including today's revolutionary leaders, have been taught that description as a meaningful portrait of an ideal leader. The text is a guide to western man's ideas about power and leadership as well as a manual on the tactics of Jesus.

The view offered here does not concern itself with the spiritual message of Jesus or his religious ideas as expressed metaphorically in his words and life. This is a description of how he organized and dealt with people.

A Man Alone

According to the gospels, when Jesus stepped into public life he was alone and unknown. The task he faced was to form a movement and to establish himself as *the* religious leader of a populace welded to a disciplined religious establishment whose leaders held the weapons of state power and operated with a body of compulsory laws controlling every individual from birth to death. Also ready to oppose any movement which might disturb the status quo were the conservative rich and the occupying Romans who wished a peaceful colony and ruthlessly exterminated revolutionists. Faced with such opposition, as formidable as any offered to mass movement leaders in this century, it would not have been surprising if Jesus had caused no more than a ripple in the social stream.

Although Jesus was alone, there were many factors on his side and like any great leader he skillfully used the forces available to him. First of all, the population was discontented. Not only was there an excessive weight of poverty and oppression but Roman taxation removed essentials as well as the surplus from this defeated country. The people also faced a priestly hierarchy made up of families which were exploitive and were maintained in power by the occupying Roman colonists. As in Russia where the Bolsheviks built upon hunger and military defeat, and in Germany where the Nazis made use of defeat and despair, the populace had little to lose by any change.

Jesus also lived at a time when the power structure was not unified but divided. The geographical division after the death of Herod had left conflict and resentment, the wealthy class and the priests had their differences, the priestly hierarchy was in internal conflict, and the Romans were sufficiently hated to make a cleavage between the governor and the populace. The establishment could not offer a united front against a bid for power.

Jesus also had on his side the mythology of the time. There was a persistent myth among the people that all difficulties could be magically alleviated by the Lord or by a Messiah who would relieve all misery, strike down all enemies, and place the tribes of Israel in power over the seventy-seven nations of the earth. With the appearance of a prophet, the hope could rise again that a deliverer had arrived. At the time Jesus stepped into the public road, there seems to have been an accepted general belief that a single man could arrive and put everything right.

Becoming Known

When Jesus appeared he was outside the pale of organizational power since he was not rich, nor a member of the religious hierarchy, nor a Roman. Riches and Roman citizenship were not available to him, but in Judaism a man could rise from low to high estate by following a religious life. That is the path Jesus chose. We do not know how he lived prior to his adult years, but when he appeared in public it was as a religious prophet.

Although an unknown cannot easily become known, Jesus was able to bring himself to the attention of the populace by using a popular tradition. People would listen to, and respect, wandering religious speakers who spoke in the streets. Such men usually condemned the cities and the hypocritical clerics who lived soft lives. Jesus stepped into this traditional pattern and spoke throughout the land — in the synagogues and in the fields, wherever the people would listen. His apparent poverty was not a handicap to the prophet's path and in fact could be defined as a virtue. The prophetic tradition was also helpful if one wished to gain a reputation before too much opposition was aroused. The state and the priestly hierarchy were accustomed to criticism within the prophet framework so that by custom a man could be heard without being immediately extinguished.

To become known in such a society, it was not only necessary to travel and to speak wherever an audience would listen, but it was necessary to speak in a certain sort of way. If one said only what was orthodox, the crowds would not listen. They could hear the proper ideas from the established religious leaders. Yet to speak and say what was unorthodox meant the risk of losing an audience by antagonizing a people devoted to an established religion which was built into their lives. Those who say that Jesus did not call for a new religion are right logically as well as according to the gospels; the populace undoubtedly would not have listened to him if he had done so. Throughout his public life Jesus managed to call attention to himself as an authority who was presenting new ideas. At the same time, he defined what he said as proper orthodoxy. He achieved this feat in two ways: first, he insisted that he was not suggesting a change and then he called for a change, and second he insisted that the ideas he was presenting were not deviations from the established religion but a more true expression of the ideas of that religion. Both of these tactics are typically used by leaders of mass movements who must, for strategic reasons, define what they do as orthodox while making the changes necessary to establish a power position. For example, Lenin supported the principle of majority rule, but he insisted that the minority was really the majority. Similarly, he argued that permitting only a single political party was a truer expression of democracy because that party represented the proletarian majority (even though it was a minority).

The skill of Jesus in calling for conformity and change simultaneously is best expressed in his discussion of the Law and its demands. The laws of religion, the civil laws, and customs were synonymous so that, when discussing the Law, Jesus was dealing with the central aspect of everyone's life. He says:

> Think not that I am come to destroy the law, or the prophets: I am not come to destroy but to fulfill . . . whosoever therefore shall break one of these least commandments, and shall teach men so, he shall be called the least in the kingdom of heaven: but whosoever shall do and teach them, the same shall be called great in the kingdom of heaven. (Matt. 5:17, 19.)

If Jesus had conformed to this teaching, no one could have had the slightest objection to what he might have said. He would have been collecting followers for the establishment rather than himself. However, he then proceeds to offer himself as *the* authority by providing major revisions of the Law. He says:

> Ye have heard that it was said by them of old time, Thou shalt not kill; and whosoever shall kill shall be in danger of the judgment: But I say unto you, That whosoever is angry with his brother without a cause shall be in danger of the judgment: and whosoever shall say to his brother, Raca, shall be in danger of the council: but whosoever shall say, Thou fool, shall be in danger of hell fire. (Matt. 5:21, 22.)

One could hardly consider this anything but a basic revision of the Law. For one thing, by emphasizing anger as criminal he is saying that men should be punished for their thoughts as well as their deeds, a major innovation. He also suggests arrest for calling someone stupid and hell for calling him a fool. In the same way he revises the law of adultery:

> Ye have heard that it was said by them of old time, Thou shalt not commit adultery: But I say unto you, That whosoever looketh on a woman to lust after her hath committed adultery with her already in his heart. (Matt. 5:27, 28.)

The law of divorce is also revised:

> It hath been said, Whosoever shall put away his wife, let him give her a writing of divorcement: but I say unto you, That whosoever shall put away his wife, saving for the cause of fornication, causeth her to commit adultery: and whosoever shall marry her that is divorced committeth adultery. (Matt. 5:31, 32.)

And so is the procedure for taking oaths:

> Again, ye have heard that it hath been said by them of old time, Thou shalt not forswear thyself, but shalt perform unto the Lord thine oaths: But I say unto you, Swear not at all; neither by heaven; for it is God's throne: Nor by earth; for it is his footstool: neither by Jerusalem; for it is the city of the great King. Neither shalt thou swear by thy head, because thou canst not make one hair white or black. But let your communication be, Yea, yea; Nay, nay: for whatsoever is more than these cometh of evil. (Matt. 5:33–37.)

Additionally he revised the law of revenge, the procedures for giving charity, the method of prayer, and the way to fast. In fact, little is left of the established Law when he has redesigned it—after stating that he has not come to change a letter of the Law. Contrasting himself with the established authorities on the Law, he implies they are hardly worth listening to by saying:

> For I say unto you, That except your righteousness shall

exceed the righteousness of the scribes and Pharisees, ye shall
in no case enter into the kingdom of heaven. (Matt. 5:20.)

By calling for conformity to the Law, Jesus disarms opposition. By then redesigning the Law, he sets himself up as an equal
in power and authority to the entire religious establishment of
the state. It is not surprising that his listeners were

astonished at his doctrine: For he taught them as one having
authority, and not as the scribes. (Matt. 5:28, 29.)

The culture he inherited provided Jesus with a special opportunity to be an authority. In Israel it was assumed that the
laws men should follow had been laid out in the beginning and
one could only discover and interpret them. In other cultures,
in contrast, it is possible to see similar laws as the product of
consensus; men make the laws which people should follow. When
it is assumed that laws exist independent of man and one can
only discover what they are, a single individual can speak with
as much authority as an establishment because he can claim to
have discovered the true law. He can request a change by saying
his opponents have deviated from the true laws of the religion.
(Contemporary mass movement leaders have used the "laws of
historical development" in the same way—the truth is to be
discovered.)

Throughout his career Jesus attacked the leaders of the establishment consistently and cleverly, but he based his attack
within their religious framework. He said they deviated from the
true religion, setting himself up as the authority on what the true
religion should be. Nowhere in the gospels is there a compliment
by Jesus for any established religious leader, except those long
deceased. The nearest to a compliment he pays is to his fellow
and competing prophet, John. He says:

Verily I say unto you, Among them that are born of women
there hath not risen a greater than John the Baptist: [but he

adds] notwithstanding he that is least in the kingdom of heaven
is greater than he. (Matt. 11:11.)

To become known and develop a following, it was not only
necessary for Jesus to say that which would arouse his audience,
but he must also offer something which would make his name
known rapidly throughout the land. The reputation of Jesus as
a healer gave him his greatest notoriety. It is the nature of the
healing trade to strike a deep chord of wishful thinking in people.
Legends build quickly and success in healing breeds belief in
success and therefore more success. Certainly once a man had
a reputation as a healer a touch of his robes could produce cures
(which was why a guard was maintained to keep the masses of
diseased people from touching the robes of the Roman emperor).
Whether Jesus had more than usual skill we cannot know, but
the fact that he chose to be a healer demonstrates his ability to
select a way to become immediately famous. Perhaps no other
device would have spread his name so quickly, particularly in
an age when medicine was inadequate against disease and people
were emotionally wrought up over the possession of devils. Since
illness knows no class, this reputation also gave him access to the
rich and he was begged for his assistance by the leader of a
synagogue, a wealthy man, and a Roman centurion. Even the
noble Herod Antipas welcomed him because of that reputation,
although Jesus would not please him with a cure. (Luke 23.) Not
only did Jesus extend his reputation by healing, but he proceeded
in such a way that opposition to him could not easily develop.
He did not brag about his cures and so arouse investigations or
resistance; instead he advised his patients to keep the cure secret.
(Mark 5.) Since no one who has been cured of a lifelong distress
is likely to, or will find it possible to, conceal the cure, the result
was to have the cure broadcast by others so that only the statements of others could be refuted. He might be accused of indirectly bragging at least once. When the messengers came from
John to ask if he was the one who is to come, Jesus said:

> Go and show John again those things which ye do hear and
> see: The blind receive their sight, and the lame walk, the lepers
> are cleansed, and the deaf hear, the dead are raised up, and
> the poor have the gospel preached to them. (Matt. 11:4, 5.)

There is yet one other power tactic which can be used by an
unknown if he wishes to be known quickly, although it is a way
which has its own risks. If a man wishes to be thought of as an
equal, or a superior, to a powerful opponent, he can make audacious personal attacks upon him. The more audacious the attack,
the more prominent does the attacker become if it is widely
known. It is common for leaders of mass movements, no matter
how small their following initially, to oppose audaciously prominent authorities as if they are on the same plane with them. Jesus
not only attacked the established religious leaders by saying such
things as, "Ye serpents, ye generation of vipers, how can ye escape
the damnation of hell?" (Matt. 23:33) but he made a physical
assault on the religious hierarchy when he attacked the money-
changers in the temple.

Building an Organization

Jesus utilized the prophet tradition but he differed sharply
from other prophets in his methods. A typical prophet was John
the Baptist who came out of the wilderness wearing animal skins
and calling upon everyone to repent. Such men took a high moral
tone in their proclamations and lived ascetic lives, standing alone
as a kind of conscience of the multitude. Transient followers
might be attracted to them out of curiosity or because they sought
a touch of divinity, but the prophet was essentially a solitary man
who lived outside of society.

Jesus, on the contrary, began his public career by choosing
men to join him in his movement. Clearly he was a man building
an organization. One of his first acts was to recruit a cadre who
would recruit others. As Matthew puts it, Jesus

saw two brethren, Simon called Peter, and Andrew his brother, casting a net into the sea: for they were fishers. And he
saith unto them, Follow me, and I will make you fishers of
men. (Matt. 4:18, 19.)

Jesus certainly had twelve in his organization and he is
reported to have had more than seventy (which is an organization
of some size). As Luke puts it:

> After these things the Lord appointed another seventy
> also, and sent them two and two before his face into every city
> and place, whither he himself would come. (Luke 10:1.) And
> the seventy returned again with joy, saying, Lord, even the
> devils are subject unto us through thy name. (Luke 10:17.)

In the selection of this elite, Jesus did not recruit among the
members of the establishment but from the lower strata of the
population where he was gathering his following. When he re-
cruited his men, he asked of them what is now typically asked
of any small revolutionary cadre. They had to give up everything
related to ambition in the society as it was and abandon all other
commitments to others, including family ties, when they joined
him. As he said:

> He that loveth father or mother more than me is not worthy
> of me: and he that loveth son or daughter more than me is
> not worthy of me. (Matt. 10:37.)

To the young man who wished to do his filial duty and bury
his father, he said "Let the dead bury their dead." (Luke 9:60.)
He did not ask more of the others than of himself in this regard.
When he was told his mother and brothers were outside and
wished to speak to him he said:

> Who is my mother? and who are my brethren? And he
> stretched forth his hand toward his disciples, and said, Behold
> my mother and my brethren! (Matt. 12:48, 49.)

Mass movement leaders characteristically follow the example of Jesus and require that their followers give up all allegiance to others, including their families.*

Jesus specifically gave his men the status of an elite. He said to them:

> Because it is given unto you to know the mysteries of the kingdom of heaven, but to them it is not given. (Matt. 13:11.)

And he said:

> Verily I say unto you, Whatsoever ye shall bind on earth shall be bound in heaven: and whatsoever ye shall loose on earth shall be loosed in heaven. (Matt. 18:18.)

He gave them authority to heal the sick, raise the dead, cleanse lepers, and cast out devils, all the activities which gave himself fame. He welded them to himself with promises. When Peter asked what they would gain by following him, he said:

> Verily I say unto you, That ye which have followed me, in the regeneration when the Son of man shall sit in the throne of his glory, ye shall sit upon twelve thrones, judging the twelve tribes of Israel. (Matt. 19:28.)

It would seem evident that his promise to his followers included what they would achieve when he came to power and not merely what they might gain from listening to him, as they might to a teacher. Jesus also effectively threatened his men, saying:

> But whosoever shall deny me before men, him will I also deny before my Father which is in heaven. (Matt. 10:33.)

And he kept his men unsure and so more actively dedicated in

---

*Eric Hoffer, *The True Believer*, New York, Harper, 1950.

following him by raising the doubt whether they were finally
acceptable to him:

> Not every one that saith unto me, Lord, Lord, shall enter
> into the kingdom of heaven: but he that doeth the will of my
> Father which is in heaven. Many will say to me in that day,
> Lord, Lord, have we not prophesied in thy name? and in thy
> name have cast out devils? and in thy name done many won-
> derful works? And then will I profess unto them, I never knew
> you: depart from me, ye that work iniquity. (Matt. 7:21-23.)

Jesus used the persecution by outsiders as a tactic for bringing
unity to his group, as is now done by all revolutionary leaders.
He said:

> Behold, I send you forth as sheep in the midst of wolves:
> be ye therefore wise as serpents, and harmless as doves. But
> beware of men: for they will deliver you up in the councils,
> and they will scourge you in their synagogues. (Matt. 10:16,
> 17.)

> And the brother shall deliver up the brother to death, and the
> father the child: and the children shall rise up against their
> parents, and cause them to be put to death. And ye shall be
> hated of all men for my name's sake: but he that endureth to
> the end shall be saved. (Matt. 10:21, 22.)

Not only does he call for unity against persecution from
outside, but he adds to this a threat of what they should really
fear when he says:

> Fear not them which kill the body, but are not able to kill
> the soul: but rather fear him which is able to destroy both soul
> and body in hell. (Matt. 26:28.)

The instructions of Jesus to his disciples indicate a deliberate
effort to develop a following among the poor. When he sent his
men out, he told them,

> Provide neither gold, nor silver, nor brass in your purses,
> nor script for your journey, neither two coats, neither shoes,
> nor yet staves: for the workman is worthy of his meat. (Matt.
> 10:9, 10.)

Since he sent them out to proclaim the kingdom of Heaven, heal the sick, raise the dead, cleanse the lepers, and cast out devils, this instruction to go as poor men without money or a second coat seems peculiar. He is not merely advising them to live an ascetic life but instructing them how to appear when dealing with the multitude. One can take a second coat and still cure, but one cannot win followers among the poor with money or a second coat or even shoes.

Jesus trained his cadre in his methods, but he managed, as any good leader should, not to be surpassed by them. He put them in their places by criticizing their obtuseness in not understanding his parables, their inability to do miracles and heal properly, and their jealousy over who will be first with him and highest in rank when success comes. As a matter of fact, there is no compliment paid by Jesus to any of his followers. The nearest thing is his comment when Peter has suggested "Thou art the Christ, the Son of the Living God." Jesus replies:

> Blessed art thou, Simon Barjona: for flesh and blood hath
> not revealed it unto thee, but my father which is in heaven.
> And I say also unto thee, That thou art Peter, and upon this
> rock I will build my church: and the gates of hell shall not
> prevail against it. (Matt. 16:17, 18.)

However, Jesus then says that he must go to Jerusalem and be put to death and when Peter protests, Jesus says,

> Get thee behind me, Satan: Thou art an offense unto me:
> For thou savourest not the things that be of God, but those
> of men. (Matt. 16:23.)

Whether Jesus is justified in criticizing the obtuseness of his men is open to interpretation. However, the gospels indicate that he did not succeed in training them to be as skillful as he was at handling criticism. Whenever Jesus was attacked or questioned, he responded with attack or question, always putting his critics in their places and never using defensive behavior. Yet after his death when his men were speaking and amazing a crowd by "speaking in tongues," a critic said, contemptuously, "These men are full of new wine." But Peter, standing up with the eleven, lifted up his voice, and said unto them, "Ye men of Judaea, and all ye that dwell at Jerusalem, be this known unto you, and hearken to my words: For these are not drunken, as ye suppose, seeing it is but the third hour of the day." (Acts 2:13–15.) That was hardly a reply worthy of the master.

Collecting a Following

If a man seeks power in a society he must usually work his way up within the current established political framework. It could be argued that Jesus did not seek political power because he made no attempt to seek a position within the religious hierarchy, just as he emphasized the more supernatural "Son of Man" rather then the more political "Son of David." However, to say that Jesus did not seek political power because he did not seek a priestly office is to overlook the new strategy he introduced into the world. It is like saying that Lenin did not seek power because he did not join the Czar's court. Since Jesus, revolutionary leaders have learned to bypass entirely the current political establishment and build an independent movement. Such leaders do not seek acceptance and advancement within the establishment, they appeal for their support among the dispossessed of society.

Jesus was the first leader to lay down a program for building a following among the poor and the powerless. His basic tactic was to define the poor as more deserving of power than anyone else and so to curry their favor. With the first statements of his public life he pointed out that the poor were blessed. Speaking to an audience of the poor and discontented, he called them the salt of the earth, the light of the world, and he announced that the meek would inherit the earth. Consistently he attacked the rich, saying they would have difficulty entering his kingdom, and speaking to audiences composed of the last he emphasized that the last would be first. Not only did he send his elite out as poor men, but he himself gained a reputation for wining and dining with the outcasts of respectable society. Nowhere does he criticize the poor, but only the rich, the learned, and the priestly establishment.

The promises of Jesus to the poor have been used as a model by later mass movement leaders. He promised a paradise in some ill-defined future if only they followed him.* Similarly, the Bolsheviks offered a classless society and Hitler a thousand year Reich. Jesus even implied that the day was in the not too distant future by saying:

> Verily I say unto you, That there be some of them that stand here, which shall not taste of death, till they have seen the kingdom of God come with power. (Mark 10:1.)

Jesus also offered the sufferers opportunity to suffer for a good cause by pointing out to them:

> Blessed are ye, when men shall revile you, and persecute you, and shall say all manner of evil against you falsely, for my sake. Rejoice, and be exceeding glad: for great is your reward in heaven: for so persecuted they the prophets which were before you. (Matt. 5:11, 12.)

As every revolutionary leader now does, Jesus offered to take all problems upon himself when he said:

---

*As Hoffer puts it, "In all ages men have fought most desperately for beautiful cities yet to be built and gardens yet to be planted." Op. cit. p. 73.

Come unto me, all ye that labour and are heavy laden, and I will give you rest. Take my yoke upon you, and learn of me; for I am meek and lowly in heart; and ye shall find rest unto your souls. For my yoke is easy, and my burden is light. (Matt. 11:28–30.)

While offering his yoke, Jesus advised the populace that if they heard his words and acted upon them they would be like the man who built his house upon a rock, and if they did not they would be like the man who is foolish enough to build his house on sand so that it comes crashing down. (Matt. 7:24–27.)

It would seem evident that Jesus was establishing long-range plans for his organization. If he was building the foundation of an organization, as later revolutionary leaders have done, he would need to put his hopes in separating the young from ties to their parents and the current establishment. Leaders of mass movements have typically emphasized reaching the young people. (They have also used the young against dissidents among their own followers, as Mao Tse-Tung did with his Red Guards.) When Jesus rebukes his disciples for keeping children from him, he says:

Suffer little children, and forbid them not to come unto me: for of such is the kingdom of heaven. (Matt. 19:14.)*

Jesus may or may not have seen the hope of his organization in the next generation, but certainly he called for the breaking of family ties and the pitting of the young against their elders. The conservative force of the family is an impediment to any mass movement, and only after becoming the establishment does a revolutionary group call for family solidity. The precedent for twentieth century movements' separating the follower from his family resides in the statements of Jesus when he says:

*The translation in *The English Bible: New Testament* (Oxford Univ. Press, 1961) is " . . . the kingdom of Heaven belongs to such as these."

> Think not that I am come to send peace on earth: I came
> not to send peace, but a sword. For I am come to set a man
> at variance against his father, and daughter against her moth-
> er, and the daughter in law against her mother in law. And
> a man's foes shall be they of his own household. (Matt.
> 10:34–36.)

Revolutionists in general say that they are not to be followed because of their person but because of what their person represents; they indicate that as individuals they do not take full credit, or blame, for what they say, because they are only spokesmen for a greater force. Jesus insisted he did not speak for himself but only expressed the will of his heavenly Father. He defined opposition to himself as opposition to the Lord, and he inhibited resistance to himself, or accusations of self-aggrandizement, by consistently pointing out that he was a mere instrument. However, he also defined himself as the *only* instrument which could interpret the heavenly father correctly.

The leaders of all revolutionary movements have learned to define themselves as leading a movement that will inevitably come to power. This way, the irresistible is on their side. Jesus set the precedent for this tactic when he prophesied that the Son of Man would *inevitably* appear and the kingdom of Heaven would arrive. By arguing that they are only shortening the time of arrival, or clarifying the progress of, an inevitable event, such leaders encourage recruits to accept an established fact and inhibit opponents who might fear going against the course of history.

The Major Tactical Contribution of Jesus

As the concept of power is used here, a person has achieved "power" when he has established himself as the one who is to determine what is going to happen. Power tactics are those maneuvers a person uses to give himself influence and control over his social world and so make that world more predictable. Defined thus broadly, a man has power if he can order someone to behave in a certain way, but he also has power if he can provoke someone to behave in that way. One man can order others to lift and carry him, while another might achieve the same end by collapsing. Both men are determining what is to happen in their social environment by the use of a power tactic. Many individuals appear to consider the gain of power positions more important than any subjective distress they might experience. The alcoholic who says to the bartender, "If you want me out of here, throw me out," may suffer pain and indignity, but *he* determines the outcome of the interchange. It is even possible to determine what is to happen from beyond the grave, as victims of wills and those whose intimates have committed suicide will testify. When we examine the tactics of Jesus, it is useful to consider power tactics defined this broadly.

Many revolutionary leaders have condemned Jesus for the tactics he introduced. Their objections are not based on a study of the tactics as Jesus used them, but in the way established powers learned to use them later. For example, by the current century the establishment could remain in power if it persuaded the oppressed to look to a future life for reward. However, the use of this tactic by Jesus did not serve the establishment; it was a method for stirring up the poor. When Jesus advised his followers to expect their reward in Heaven, he did this in combination with a threat that they might burn in Hell. He was not using the promise of Heaven as a way of persuading the poor to accept their misery, but as a promise that if they followed him and resisted the establishment they would achieve Heaven; if they followed the establishment they would not. As he put it:

> The Son of man shall send forth his angels, and they shall gather out of his kingdom all things that offend, and them which do iniquity; And shall cast them into a furnace of fire: there shall be wailing and gnashing of teeth. Then shall the righteous shine forth as the son in the kingdom of their Father. Who hath ears to hear, let him hear. (Matt. 13:41–43.)

He warned them that the judgment would take them un-
awares, and he drew a sharp distinction between those who were
with him and those who were against him. He said:

> He that is not with me is against me: and he that gathereth
> not with me scattereth. (Luke 11:23.)

The condemnation of Christians for using the tactic of weakness also indicates a misunderstanding of the strategic position
of Jesus. While Bolsheviks might argue that force must be met
by force, and when Hitler said that terror must be met with equal
terror, they were adapting to a quite different situation. Jesus
could not possibly marshal force equal to the force of Rome or
terror equal to the offerings of the establishment. A leader at that
time might achieve sporadic riots, but organized attack against
the occupying army of the Romans was futile, as Roman execu-
tions regularly demonstrated. Insofar as the Romans were supporting the religious establishment and permitting it authority
over the people, whose who opposed the church risked being
exterminated. In this situation Jesus developed the surrender
tactic, a procedure which has been used by the powerless in the
face of the invincible to this day.

The Surrender Tactic

At one point Jesus contrasts his lot with the beasts of the field
and the birds of the air, and it is worthwhile to compare his tactics
as well. As with man, animals form social groups with a hierarchical power structure and inevitably there are struggles for power
as a revolutionist attempts to climb and the established leaders
oppose him. Among the many tactics used by animals in this
struggle, the one most relevant to the study of Jesus is the "surrender tactic" reportedly used by certain beasts of the field and
birds of the air. When two wolves are in a fight and one is about
to be killed, the defeated wolf will suddenly lift his head and bare

his throat to his opponent. The opponent becomes incapacitated and he cannot kill him as long as he is faced with this tactic. Although he is the victor, the vanquished is controlling his behavior merely by standing still and offering his vulnerable jugular vein. The turkey too when faced with a stronger opponent will stretch out his neck along the ground, assuming a helpless posture, and an opponent from his species cannot attack and kill him. This connection between Jesus and animal behavior is also made by Lorenz. Commenting on the lesson to be learned from the behavior of wolves, he says, "I at least have extracted from it a new and deeper understanding of a wonderful and often misunderstood saying from the Gospel, which hitherto had only awakened in me the feelings of strong opposition. 'And unto him that smiteth thee on the one cheek offer also the other.' (Luke 6:29.) A wolf has enlightened me; not so that your enemy may strike you again do you turn the other cheek toward him, but to make him unable to do it."*

Although it might be argued that the "surrender tactic" is merely a device by animals to suffer defeat without being extinguished and man has used this tactic in his wars, it is also possible to see the procedure as a way of determining what is to happen. You cannot defeat a helpless opponent; if you strike him and your blows are unreturned, you can only suffer feelings of guilt and exasperation as well as doubt about who is the victor. This tactic has been proved effective by weeping wives and by anxious parents who find that helplessness will enforce their directives more tyrannically than giving orders. The extreme tactic of threat of suicide falls in a similar category.

The surrender tactic, or turning the other cheek, has its risks as well as its triumphs. It would seem to be a tactic which either wins or provokes murderous extermination, as the early Christians learned. The fact that the three foremost exponents of this procedure, Jesus, Gandhi, and Martin Luther King died violent deaths, just as surely as if they had lived by the sword, would

---

*Lorenz, K., *King Solomon's Ring*, New York, Thomas Y. Crowell, 1952.

not seem accidental. (The debt of Gandhi to Jesus for the tactic of nonviolent resistance is obvious. Gandhi reports that in his early years he read the Sermon on the Mount, "which went straight to my heart."* Whether he developed this surrender tactic more fully than Jesus we cannot really know because we do not have sufficient information from Jesus while we do have a great deal from Gandhi.) It would appear that the use of meekness to determine what is to happen in a power struggle works most effectively if there is a threat of violence in the background to support the meek tactic. What success there has been with Negro nonviolence can be seen as a product of the fear of whites of more violent uprisings if they assassinated many of these young people.

Throughout his public life Jesus preached, although he rarely practiced, the tactic of turning the other cheek, loving one's enemies and praying for them, and forgiving those who wrong you seventy times seven times (which should lead any opponent to capitulation). How explicit he was in describing this as a strategical concept rather than a religious tenet is evident in a single sentence where he advised a procedure which has been used by the downtrodden in the face of invincible authority ever since. Sometimes it is called the army game, since the lowliest private can win a power struggle with his highest superior if he merely does more than he is told. If a recalcitrant soldier is told to mop the floor, he not only can mop it but be dutifully mopping it eight hours later. (The authors of a psychiatric paper describe a soldier who managed to find a mop with only one strand for his weapon in this struggle.) His superiors will be both furious and incapacitated since they cannot punish him for doing what he is told. Jesus expressed this tactic neatly in his general discussion of the use of the helpless strategy in the face of authority. He says:

> Ye have heard that it hath been said, An eye for an eye
> and a tooth for a tooth: But I say unto you, That ye resist not

*Gandhi's *Autobiography*. Washington, Public Affairs Press, 1948, quoted in *The Gandhi Reader*, edited by H. A. Jack, New York, Grove Press, 1956, page 3.

evil: but whosoever shall smite thee on thy right cheek, turn
to him the other also. And if any man will sue thee at the law,
and take away thy coat, let them have thy cloak also. And
whosoever shall compel thee to go a mile, go with him twain.
(Matt. 5:38–41.)

Whether Jesus originated the surrender tactic appears doubt-
ful, but certainly he codified it and stated it most explicitly. It
is reported that the Jews once vanquished Pilate by just such a
tactic during the time of Jesus. When Pilate was first made
governor, he set up his headquarters in Caesarea and put up the
banners of Tiberius in Jerusalem. The Jews protested these
banners in their holy city and came in a mob to Caesarea. Pilate
surrounded the mob with his troops and told them that if they
did not disperse he would kill them all. The unarmed Jews "flung
themselves in a body on the ground, extended their necks, and
exclaimed that they were ready to die rather than to transgress
the Law."* The banners of Caesar were taken down in Jerusalem.

That this was a deliberate tactic devised by Jesus rather than
a personal philosophy is suggested by the fact that he never turned
the other cheek himself. Typically with adversaries, such as the
scribes and Pharisees who criticized him, Jesus not only answered
criticism with criticism but reviled and threatened them. When
the Pharisees criticized his men because they ate corn on the
Sabbath, Jesus pointed out that David ate the consecrated loaves
and besides the Son of Man is Lord of the Sabbath day. When
they said he cured by the devil, he called them a generation of
vipers, and when they inquired why his disciples did not wash
their hands before they ate he called them hypocrites. (Matt. 15.)
These are not meek responses and Jesus typically dealt with his
opponents by responding with a question or with an attack and
not passive resistance. In fact, Jesus never forgave anyone who
wronged or criticized him, although he forgave those who had

---

*Josephus, War ii. 169–177 in C. K. Barrett (Ed.), *The New Testament Background:
Selected Documents*, New York, Harper and Row, 1961, p. 124.

wronged others. On the cross he offered a general forgiveness of everyone when he said, "Father forgive them; for they know not what they do." But when offered an opportunity to forgive in a personal encounter he always declined. As a major example, he might have forgiven Judas who betrayed him, but instead Jesus said, "but woe unto that man by whom the Son of man is betrayed! it had been good for that man if he had not been born." (Matt. 26:24.)*

The Climax of the Struggle for Power

The examination of Jesus as a tactician not only increases our understanding of the nature of power struggles, but this perspective also suggests a possible resolution of some of the contradictions in the gospels. The gospel authors offer more confusion about the final days of Jesus than any part of his life. In their determination to prove him innocent they neglect to state what charges were made against him, and their attempts to fit his actions into complicated prophecies about the Messiah compound the confusion.

When Jesus went into the final struggle he arranged a situation where there was no hope of compromise. He condemned the clergy, he condemned the temple, and finally he made a physical assault upon the temple. Although Jesus took care not to call for open rebellion against the priestly hierarchy, he thoroughly discredited them. As he put it:

> The scribes and the Pharisees sit in Moses' seat: All there-
> fore whatsoever they bid you observe, that observe and do;

---

*It is possible that Jesus was making a philosophical statement about offenders rather than a personal comment on Judas. Durkheim suggested that every society needs deviants so that the remainder of the society can know how to behave with each other. Jesus anticipated him by saying, "Woe unto the world because of offences! for it must needs be that offences come; but woe to that man by whom the offence cometh!" (Matt. 18:7.)

but do not ye after their works: for they say, and do not. For they bind heavy burdens and grievous to be borne, and lay them on men's shoulders; but themselves will not move them with one of their fingers. (Matt. 23:2-4.)

Woe unto you, scribes and Pharisees, hypocrites! for ye shut up the kingdom of heaven against men: for ye neither go in yourselves, neither suffer ye them that are entering to go in. (Matt. 23:13.)

Jesus did not merely criticize, he took action. He made an audacious assault on the temple when he entered it and upset the tables of the money changers and the dealers in sacrificial animals. Since an essential part of the economy of the temple was the sale of animals and changing of money, this was no minor assault. Again, his attack demonstrates his skill as a tactician, for he chose his opponents' most vulnerable area for his attack. He did not violate the altar or intrude upon the Holy of Holies — he focused on the commercial aspect of the temple, saying they were turning a house of prayer into a robbers' cave. By this kind of public attack he could win immediate fame throughout the city while not giving his opposition an advantage. It was awkward for the priesthood to retaliate against him for his violent ways because he was quoting their own scripture to them, attacking a point difficult to defend.

Jesus not only condemned the establishment, but he offered himself as alternative; he even points out that he could tear that temple down and rebuild it in three days.

The position Jesus had taken was too extreme: the establishment had to take action against him if it were to survive. Apparently they sought to lay hands on him but "they feared the multitude" (Matt. 21:46); and there was an attempt to stone him but he escaped. The only remaining alternative was to arrest him.

Despite the confusion in the gospels about the final days of Jesus, there are several points which appear clear:

1. Over the objections of his followers, Jesus insisted that he was going to Jerusalem to be arrested. When he arrived in that holy city, he behaved in such an extreme manner that he forced

his arrest. He either arranged that the arresting officers find him, or at least he waited patiently for them to come to him. It is possible to interpret the betrayal by Judas as arranged by Jesus. Jesus says "one of you shall betray me" and when asked who it is:

> Jesus answered, He it is, to whom I shall give a sop, when I have dipped it. And when he had dipped the sop, he gave it to Judas Iscariot, the son of Simon. And after the sop Satan entered into him. Then said Jesus unto him, that thou doest, do quickly. (John 13:26, 27.)

2. He was tried and condemned to death by the Sanhedrin and was passed to the Roman governor for execution.

3. Pilate declined to execute him since he found no evidence that he had broken Roman law.

4. Pilate turned to the populace for a decision and the crowd called for the death of Jesus.

Up until the time of his trial, the behavior of Jesus was consistent with various possible interpretations. Given his aggressive behavior and his willingness to be arrested, at least the following interpretations appear reasonable. (a) He was actually the Messiah and must therefore go through the prophetic pattern of being handed over to his enemies and executed. (b) He was sacrificing himself for the sins of the world as part of the Messianic pattern, and this was his individual choice. (c) He went mad, as Shaw suggests and Schweitzer denies, and decided that he was the Messiah and must die so that the kingdom of Heaven could immediately arrive.* Or (d) he did not intend to die but wished to be arrested because he was finally pitting himself and the strength of his organization in a final power struggle with the establishment.

The behavior of Jesus *after* his arrest was of such a nature that only the last of these interpretations appears to fit the facts.

---

*Shaw, B., preface to *Androcles and the Lion*, Baltimore, Penguin, 1951, and Schweitzer, A., *The Psychiatric Study of Jesus*, Boston, Beacon Press, 1948.

After permitting, or arranging, the arrest, he made it almost impossible for the establishment to condemn him and execute him. If he merely wished to be executed as part of the Messianic prophecy or to sacrifice himself for the sins of the world, he could have announced that he was the Messiah, opposed Roman rule, and his execution would have been routine. If he had gone mad and sought to sacrifice himself in a suicidal manner, he similarly would have behaved in a provocative way and made the execution simple. Yet he did no such thing. He refused to speak, refused to say that he was the Messiah and refused to oppose Rome. In fact he behaved in such a way that his execution appeared impossible — after amiably surrendering himself into the hands of the establishment.

After he was arrested:

> Now the chief of priests, and elders, and all the council, sought false witness against Jesus, to put him to death; But found none: Yea, though many false witnesses came, yet found they none. (Matt. 26:59, 60.)

In this situation Jesus did not curse and revile the scribes and Pharisees or even defend himself and assert his authority. He said nothing through many hours of interrogation and futile calling of witnesses. Matthew continues:

> At the last came two false witnesses, And said, This fellow said, I am able to destroy the temple of God, and to build it in three days. And the high priest arose and said unto him, Answerest thou nothing? what is it which these witnesses against thee? But Jesus held his peace. (Matt. 26:60–63.)

It is only when provoked that Jesus finally speaks, and then his answer is ambiguous:

> And the high priest answered and said unto him, I adjure thee by the living God, that thou tell us whether thou be the Christ, the Son of God. Jesus saith unto him, Thou hast said:

nevertheless I say unto you, Hereafter shall ye see the Son of man sitting on the right hand of power, and coming in the clouds of heaven. Then the high priest rent his clothes, saying, He hath spoken blasphemy what further need have we of witnesses? Behold, now ye have heard his blasphemy. What think ye? They answered and said, He is guilty of death. (Matt. 26:63–66.)

For Jesus to say, "Thou has said" is not the same as saying, "Yes I am." Only one of the four testament writers has him admit he is the Messiah, and all agree that this happened after he remained silent throughout the proceedings. Mark has him say "I am: and ye shall see the son of man sitting on the right hand of power, and coming in the clouds of heaven." (Mark 14:62.) Luke gives him the reply "Ye say that I am" (Luke 22:70) and John does not mention the matter at all. When Jesus says "Thou hast said" the high priest apparently receives the statement as synonymous with "I am." Yet when Jesus makes the same reply to Pilate, it is apparently taken as a denial. Relevant to the question whether Jesus admitted he was the Messiah here or not is the fact that he never announced that he was in his whole career but it was always announced by others.

Although the actual laws of the Sanhedrin at that time are uncertain, apparently they were people of strict procedures. This is why the evidence of witnesses was necessary; usually two were required, and under the law a man could not be condemned for statements out of his own mouth. Yet the condemnation of Jesus is said to be for a crime which is unclear and it is based entirely on these brief and ambiguous statements at the end of his trial. A mystery remains. If Jesus was the Messiah who must be sacrificed, why would not satisfactory witnesses appear so that he could easily be condemned, or at least why does he not make some of the savage statements he made elsewhere, which would have brought about his easy condemnation? By remaining silent and providing only a final and ambiguous answer, Jesus made it legally impossible for them to condemn him to death: the condemnation must be done by breaking the rules and condemning him for statements out of his own mouth. It is done in a fit of pique, on impulse.

A remarkably similar situation occurs when Jesus is brought before the Roman governor. Although the establishment was given surprising autonomy for a subjected colonial people, they could not execute a man except with permission of Pilate. Once again, if Jesus was determined to be executed, he would have to persuade Pilate to give the order. Instead, he made it extremely difficult, if not impossible, for Pilate to order his execution.

Although Jesus was willing to criticize and condemn the religious establishment and the native rulers, he was extremely circumspect in his behavior with the Romans. Nowhere in the New Testament is there any statement by him which could be considered an attack on Rome, despite the antagonism of the Hebrews toward this foreign rule. Jesus did not stir up the populace against Rome, or oppose Roman taxation (although he objected to the temple tax, c.f. Matt. 17:26). At most he included the Romans among all Gentiles and put them outside the pale. He instructed his disciples to deal only with Jews, saying, "I am not sent but unto the lost sheep of the House of Israel." (Matt. 15:2.)* Although Jesus condemned the non-Jews as a class, he does not express anti-Roman statements even when his adversaries attempt to trap him into doing so by asking if tribute should be paid to Caesar. He says, "Why put me to the test, you hypocrites?" and he adds, "Render therefore to Caesar the things that are Caesar's, and to God the things that are God's." (Matt. 22:19–21.)

It is always possible that the gospels were written by writers who did not wish to antagonize Rome and therefore they did not transcribe any of his anti-Roman statements, but it is also possible

---

*In this same passage a Gentile woman asks Jesus to cure her daughter and he tells her that his food is not for dogs. The woman offers Jesus his own preferred tactic; instead of becoming angry at this rather insulting reply she turns the other cheek and says that dogs can ask for scraps that fall from the master's table. Faced with this surrender tactic, Jesus capitulates and assists her.

that Jesus did not make any. Roman power must have appeared clearly invincible and a power strategist does not directly attack invincible power, he seeks other means of undermining it.

The refusal by Jesus to oppose Rome put Pilate in a difficult position. He could not legally execute him, but if he did not he would face an uprising from an angry priesthood. By making it impossible for Pilate to condemn him, Jesus forced a squabble between Pilate and the priestly hierarchy. Finally, Pilate turned to the populace and using the excuse of releasing a prisoner on a holiday, he put the decision in their hands. The crowd decided against him.

The question of why the crowd called for the death of Jesus remains a puzzling one if he was so popular he had to be arrested secretly. Schweitzer argues that the crowd sought his death because they learned he claimed at the trial to be the Messiah and that was blasphemous.* A Catholic version has been that the crowd was packed with priests from the temple. A more crucial question is whether the episode is authentic — since it has been argued there was no tradition of a release of a prisoner on a holiday in that state. However, all aspects of the authenticity of the trial, the rules of the Sanhedrin, the power of the governor, and so on, have been endlessly debated. The actions of Jesus should have forced the priestly hierarchy to deal with him, and the Romans must have had a problem legally executing him when he had broken no Roman law. Therefore, the gospel version would seem as adequate as any other.

Let us suppose that we are in the position of Jesus prior to his arrest and we are strategists examining what we would gain and what we would lose by arranging to be arrested. Our gains and losses would be estimated in terms of the probabilities in a situation where the outcome was uncertain. The most probable outcomes, in the order in which they are most likely to happen are these:

*Schweitzer, A., *The Quest of the Historical Jesus*, New York, Macmillan, 1961.

1. The Sanhedrin, faced with no adequate witnesses and a silent victim, would be forced to release Jesus for lack of evidence. He would prove the impotence of the establishment in the face of his movement and of his aggressive statements and his physical assault on the temple.

2. The Sanhedrin might, in exasperation, break their own laws and condemn him even without evidence. They would then take him to the Roman governor for execution. Since he had been careful to break no Roman law the governor would order him released and at most scourge him. Jesus would have discredited the temple hierarchy and proven its impotence, and he would be released as a leader who could openly oppose the temple and be tolerated by Rome.

3. By chance, and therefore it could not be predicted, the unexpected might happen and Pilate would put the decision up to the crowd. With the following Jesus had built, he would be freed by the populace and triumphantly lead a popular movement which could not be defeated by the temple hierarchy.

4. The Sanhedrin might convict him illegally, Pilate might turn to the crowd and the populace might call for his death. This latter seems the least likely possibility. Yet it is the *least likely* of the probable occurrences which actually happened.

From this point of view, it would seem possible to interpret the execution of Jesus as the result of a miscalculation on his part. Who could have guessed the Sanhedrin would condemn him without evidence, that Pilate would happen to ask the crowd for a decision, and that the crowd he had never wronged would ask for his death? Even a master tactician cannot take into account all the possibilities, including chance occurrences.

When we examine the life of Jesus, we can only conclude that it would fit his character to move prematurely to gain the whole world. All the evidence indicates that Jesus was a man with a passion to determine what was to happen in his environment. The ultimate resistance to him resided in Jerusalem and he chose that place for his final struggle. His arrest occurred at a place and time of his own choosing, provoked by his actions and so determined by them. After his arrest, he behaved in such a way that his opponents were incapacitated and forced to respond on his terms; they could neither condemn him nor release him. If he miscalculated the desperateness of his opposition, he might at last have found himself in a situation where what happened was beyond his control, as indicated by his cry from the cross, "My God, my God, why has thou forsaken me?" (Matt. 27:46). Those who argue that he deliberately sought his crucifixion support the argument that Jesus was determined to control whatever happened to him. How extreme he was in this regard is illustrated by the ways he dealt with not only his disciples and his followers, but even his physical environment. When he wanted a fig from a tree and there was none, he responded as if this was an affront to a man who should determine whatever happened. He condemned the tree to be forever barren. His followers were not surprised at this action, apparently assuming it was in character; they were only surprised that he could succeed in withering the tree. Yet even though we might suspect that his plans failed on those last days, we still face the fact that if he was a man building an organization, he did not fail. The act of being executed extended his control beyond the grave, required most of mankind to bend their necks to his yoke, and fits the character of a man who would finally say, "All power is given unto me in heaven and in earth." (Matt. 28:18.)

What Was Learned from Jesus

It would seem evident that the strategies of Jesus have been the model for mass-movement leaders, the Messiahs of this century. With the decline of the Christian religion as a philosophy, the organizational tactics of Jesus came into prominence. Contemporary leaders have followed a set of procedures which can be summarized here as they were originated by Jesus.

The basic strategy of leaders of communist, fascist, black power and other mass movements, consists of seeking power outside the establishment by cultivating the people who have been neglected and powerless. This populace is the majority in the countries where mass movements have succeeded. The leader defines the poor workers and peasants as more deserving of power than any other class, and he publicly attacks the wealthy and established. If the poor are sufficiently desperate, as at a time of military defeat, the odds increase for the success of the movement.

The leader organizes a cadre he can use as "fishers of men." These disciples are selected from the population to be influenced, and they are expected to be totally devoted to the leader and his movement. They must give up all ambition in the society as it is, cut off all family ties, and abandon all group loyalties except loyalty to the party. Once they have done this, it is difficult for them to defect and abandon the movement; they have sacrificed too much and have no place to go. The leader further ties the cadre to him by emphasizing their persecution by outsiders; and he gives them a sense of mission and purpose in life. Offering practical gains in exchange for their sacrifices, the leader also offers his disciples the status of an elite within the organization and the thrones of power in the kingdom that is to come.

In his public message the leader defines his movement as one that has the benevolent purpose of saving mankind, making it difficult to resist. He also claims the movement will inevitably come to power because it represents the next step in the development of man. When appealing to the masses, the leader promises a paradise in some undefined future if they will only follow him, and he threatens misery if they do not. He puts his hope in the young who do not yet have an investment in the establishment, and he deliberately incites the young against their elders, to break the family ties that solidify the strength of the establishment.

Defining himself as one who does not seek personal power, the leader says he is fulfilling a mission at great personal sacrifice. He does not say that he should be followed for himself or that he is a great leader but more modestly says that he is merely an interpreter of the great force which will take his following into the bountiful future. However, he also defines himself as the *only* correct interpreter of that force. Willing to live with inconsistency, the leader adapts what he says to the circumstances while at the same time insisting that he is offering a clear and consistent theory as a basis for his actions.

While gathering a following, the leader publicly announces himself as an authority who is equal to the authority of the whole establishment, and he makes audacious comments and attacks on prominent leaders in the opposition. At the same time he uses a flexible strategy, answering attack with attack when this is safe and using nonviolent methods within the legal framework if the opposition is too formidable. As the final struggle comes into being, he takes a position of "no compromise" with the governing power. Since his goal is not power within the framework of the establishment, no compromise or bargaining is possible. If he succeeds, what follows is a ruthless elimination of any and all opponents.

One cannot strike for power over masses of people today without using the strategies of Jesus. No leader has been so publicized or had his sayings and actions become such a part of the thinking of crusading men. Whether Jesus was offering an original religious philosophy or not, he was an extraordinary innovator as a leader of men. Should those who have led great power struggles be enshrined in a hall of fame, the first niche belongs to the Messiah from Galilee.

THE ART OF
BEING SCHIZOPHRENIC

It is common today to hear complaints that standards are falling in every field of endeavor. Like most generalizations, this one may not be true, but certainly standards are dropping in the field of psychiatric diagnosis. Where there was once neatness and rigor, one now finds a slipshod, lacadaisical, devil-may-care lumping together of the most diverse maladies as if the need for diagnostic precision no longer existed. The most shocking example is the diagnosis of schizophrenia. At one time it was clear that a person was either schizophrenic or not, and the several species were neatly catalogued and appreciated. Today we find that the label of schizophrenia is likely to be applied to just about anyone. A passing temper tantrum by an adolescent can earn a diagnosis of schizophrenia without providing the youth any opportunity to show his true nature and abilities in this line of endeavor. Not only are the wrong sort of people included in this category, but we also find ourselves drowning in the attempts to water down the diagnosis so that just about anyone can be classed in this way. Let us face facts: what on earth is a schizoid, or worse yet a schizo-affective state? Are not such labels merely absurd compromises showing an unwillingness to keep the diagnosis clean and pure in the European, particularly the German, tradition? At this time we should review what is required of a person who truly merits this diagnosis so that we can ruthlessly eliminate the false contenders and draw a sharp line between this and other maladies. To use the term "schizophrenic" loosely for anyone who wanders in the hospital door looking befuddled betrays those individuals who have worked long and hard to achieve the disease.

The Right Sort of Family

To say that not everyone can achieve schizophrenia is to say a great deal. Today any competent diagnostician who is sifting the true schizophrenic from the chaff will include in his observation the environment of the patient. After all, to be schizophrenic it is essential that one be born into the right sort of family and if one can manage that all else may follow. However, we cannot choose our parents, they are a gift of heaven. People who have attempted schizophrenia without the correct family background have universally failed. They can erupt into psychotic-like behavior in combat or when caught in some other mad and difficult situation, but they are unable to sustain that behavior when the environment seems to right itself. The same point applies to the variety of fascinating drugs which are falsely said to induce psychosis. Not only does the drug-influence miss the essence of the experience, but the effect wears off rapidly. The occasional goat who manages to be a schizophrenic after the drug has left his system is easily separated from the sheep who go back to normal — he has come from the right sort of family and probably would have achieved schizophrenia even without the benefit of medical research.

The type of family one must come from to become schizophrenic has been extensively described in the professional journals. One can summarize these scientific reports by saying that as individuals the family members are unrecognizable on the street but bring them together and the outstanding feature is immediately apparent — a kind of formless, bizarre despair overlaid with a veneer of glossy hope and good intentions concealing a power-struggle-to-the-death coated with a quality of continual confusion.

Observing such a family one is struck by the central figure, the mother, and notes at once that the schizophrenic owes to her his flexibility and his exasperating skill in frustrating people who attempt to influence him. Just as the child in a circus family learns from his parents how to maneuver on a slack wire, so does the schizophrenic learn from his mother how to maneuver acrobatically in interpersonal relations. To achieve schizophrenia a man must have experienced a mother who has a range of behavior unequalled except by the most accomplished of actresses. She is capable when stung (which occurs when any suggestion is made to her) of weeping, promising violence, expressing condescending concern, threatening to go mad and fall apart, being kind and pious, and offering to flee the country if another word is said. This type of mother when faced with the dreadful child she has raised, is able to reply innocently that the fault lies elsewhere since she has done nothing in life for herself but everything for her child. This halo-effect is apparent in the comment of a mother who said, "A mother sacrifices, if you would be a mother yourself you would know this, like even Jesus with his mother, a mother sacrifices everything for her child."

It should be obvious that such mothers are not easy to find and probably don't represent more than 20 per cent of the females born. Yet for the true flowering of schizophrenia, even such a mother is not enough. To balance the flexibility provided by mother, the schizophrenic must have a father who will teach him to remain immovable. The father of the schizophrenic has a stubbornness unequalled among men (as well as the skill to keep a woman in the state of exasperated despair which helps mother make use of her full range of behavior). On occasions when present and sober such a father can easily say, "I am right, God in heaven knows I cannot be proven wrong, black is not white and you know it too in your heart of hearts." This sort of father is not easily found in the general population, largely because he is rarely home.

When one considers the odds that this type of uncommon man will find such an uncommon woman, and the even more astonishing odds that two such people could copulate, it is clear at once that the incidence of true schizophrenia could not be high. (Often such parents report that the copulation only occurred when one or both was asleep and that is why they had to get married, but even granting this possibility the odds against schizophrenia being common do not change appreciably.)

Finally, it is important, although not essential, that a schizophrenic have as part of his environment a certain type of brother or sister. This sibling must be the kind of person who is hated on contact — a do-gooder, a good-in-schooler, a sweet, weak, kind bastard of a sibling who can provide the contrast for the future schizophrenic by showing him up to be the complete idiot his family expects him to be.

Given this array of talent around him, one might think the individual raised in such a family constellation would inevitably achieve schizophrenia. However, this is obviously not true since all children in such families do not go clearly mad. The schizophrenic must not only have such a family, but he must hold a certain position in it and serve certain vital functions over an extended period of time. Like any artist, several hours a day of practice over many years are necessary.

Regarding his position, he must be the child the parents choose to focus upon — that special child the parents expect to be remarkable for reasons related to their own dark pasts. Whatever this particular child does is of exaggerated importance to the parents, and he soon learns that touching his nose can set off an earthquake in the family. This parental focus is sufficiently intense that when it is turned from the schizophrenic to the sibling, the sibling begins to disintegrate like a match head placed under a burning glass.

It is the primary function of the schizophrenic to be the representative failure in the family, and in that sense be remarkable. The parents feel themselves to be insignificant wretches, lost souls incapable of any human accomplishment (although many of them make rather good scientists). Therefore for their survival they must have before their eyes the schizophrenic child as an example of a worse failure so they can stand a little higher in the world by that fact. The child can fulfill this function rather easily since he need only fail at whatever he attempts. The average schizophrenic shows his artistry by achieving more than usual ability along this line, while also indicating at regular intervals that he could do quite a good job at succeeding if he wanted to, thus shining in the light of his parents' admiration while giving them sufficient cause for disappointment.

The schizophrenic is not only the focus of his parents' life, but he serves a key position in the wider morass that is the total family network. One is reminded of the vast array of tumblers who stand upon each other's shoulders, all constructed upon one man standing at the bottom holding up the entire edifice. Just as the child is caught up in the conflict between his parents, so is he in the middle of the triangular struggle between his mother and her mother, his father and his mother, and the many other cross-generational conflicts in this type of family. (When the schizophrenic sides with his mother against father, father can only protest weakly since he is joining *his* mother against his wife.)

The average schizophrenic has had a lifetime balancing conflicting family triangles, each one focused upon his every action, so that whatever he says and does in one triangle has repercussions in another. If he should please his grandparents, he will displease his parents, and should he agree with any one person he is certain to antagonize several others. Therefore the schizophrenic must learn to communicate in a way that satisfies everyone by saying one thing and disqualifying it with a conflicting statement and then indicating he didn't mean any of it anyhow. This complicated mode of adaptation makes his behavior appear rather peculiar.

The schizophrenic soon learns, of course, that he has a position of extreme power in manipulating triangles to his advantage. The importance of his skill in this essential game cannot be overemphasized. For example, one teenage schizophrenic, precocious as most schizophrenics are, said, "My parents and I are involved in the eternal triangle," and she showed her skill in this game by climbing into bed between her parents and kicking her mother out (while father protested weakly that mother should have locked the bedroom door). The schizophrenic also takes for granted what social scientists are only beginning to realize — the true disturbance in human life comes when secret coalitions occur across generations or other power hierarchies (this is The Second

Law of Human Relations). The schizophrenic is, of course, the master at cross-generation coalitions. He may decline to join his peers, but he has even been known to provoke a great-grandfather to intrude into the parental conflict.

The primary responsibility of the schizophrenic is to hold the family together. Although social scientists, even family therapists, have not yet the vaguest idea how to prevent a family from disintegrating, the schizophrenic child accomplishes this with ease. It is his duty to use his keen perception and interpersonal skill to maintain the family system in a stable state, even if that state is a mood of constant despair. His importance in this function appears on those rare occasions when the schizophrenic abandons his disease and becomes normal, succeeding in life and leaving his family. His parents at once individually collapse, losing their sense of purpose in life, and they set about to divorce (weakly apologizing to *their* parents for being more successful as parents than they were).

The schizophrenic child prevents divorce and family dissolution in a rather simple way; he provides the parents an excuse for staying together by offering himself as a problem. With minor threats of separation, he merely looks unhappy to provide mother and father with an excuse to stay together. When the parents are constantly on the verge of leaving one another, the child must present himself as a more severe problem. Such children learn quickly how to behave; a few odd mannerisms and grimaces at inappropriate moments are helpful, as well as muteness and a kind of twisting, weird waving of the hands accompanied by an occasional idiotic squeal. If of school age, the child must show that he is incapable of existing outside the family and therefore his parents must stay together and comfort him since they are his only source of life. By becoming the family problem, the child requires his parents to stay together to save him, offers himself as an excuse for their misery with each other, and he also challenges them. These parents feel they must be perfect parents. When their child behaves oddly all their determination to cure him is aroused, thus giving them further reason to continue to associate as a family.

The schizophrenic must also act quickly if the parents threaten to come closer together and be more affectionate, thereby provoking a change in the family (as well as panic in the parents). Should father almost reach out a hand to mother, the schizophrenic must promptly wet his pants, or he must say, "Oh, I want to visit Granny," thereby bringing father's mother into the scene, which always provokes an argument between parents.

When the schizophrenic is old enough to perceive that his family is culturally defiant, he begins to function as the symbol of the family's differentness. The peculiar way he chooses to express himself on this matter will drive the parents closer together and at the same time attract community attention to provide some help for the family. His technique is to use parody. Schizophrenics have long been known as the most skilled people at parody in the world, and it has been said that they parody all the worst aspects of our society. This gives them too much credit; they are merely parodying their families. For example, if the parents insist that they are devoutly religious while behaving in a most unreligious manner, the schizophrenic son will begin to grow a beard and burn holes in the palms of his hands with cigarettes. Should this not attract sufficient attention—some of these parents will consider this only playful behavior—then the schizophrenic will take to strolling about the neighborhood carrying a large cross. The parents do not always take this as action in their best interest, particularly since they have a passion for secrecy about many matters, but in such a case they can hardly accuse the child of misbehavior when he merely is being more religious than they are. In a similar way, if the parents have unsavory minds while insisting that they are terribly puritan, the schizophrenic will loudly condemn dirty words, naming them and even writing them on the front sidewalk.

The skill with which a schizophrenic calls attention to a family problem while simultaneously declining responsibility for doing this is best illustrated by his verbal comments. The ideal comment is one which is as ambiguous as mother could offer—it must reach the parents in their souls but keep them uncertain whether an outsider gets the point. For example, a schizophrenic daughter listened to her parents describe how happy this family was except for this wretched daughter, and she said, "Yes, but wouldn't you and Daddy be happier if you didn't drink so much?" Granting that this calls attention to the parents' need for help, it was also a rather unskillful and crude thrust which does not merit being called schizophrenic. This rude directness might be attributed to the daughter's faulty control of her anger. The more experienced schizophrenic can completely control the expression of his feelings and offer flattened affect even when the doctors are sticking pins into him at medical demonstrations. One can only applaud a son who sent his mother a Mother's Day card which said, "You've always been like a mother to me," and a daughter who arrived with her mother and stepfather in a psychiatrist's office and said, "Mother had to get married and now I'm here."

When the family threatens to dissolve, the schizophrenic must be willing to go to any extreme, even insane activity which brings in the neighbors and the police. It is the willingness on his part to fulfill the function of holding the family together which explains why the schizophrenic — despite his skill, wariness, and keen perception — lets himself be cast into a mental hospital. His psychotic behavior is a last resort when a family crisis has reached the point where an unresolvable breach is about to take place. This final extremity drives the parents together because of their common burden of a truly unfortunate child, forces the parents into a common front against the community which is protesting that something must be done, and lets the family make the schizophrenic the patsy for all past and present difficulties. The psychotic episode is merely a more extreme version of other behavior of the schizophrenic at times of family crisis, but this time it precipitates him into a situation which calls forth all his skill — the treatment situation. Before describing the talent necessary for the schizophrenic to survive in the hospital setting, let us summarize the training the schizophrenic has had when he arrives, his face unwashed and his hair uncombed, ready for entrance into the institution which will become his tomb.

In sum, the schizophrenic must have come from the right sort of family, with appropriate parents as models. He must have learned to manipulate and balance complicated, conflicting family triangles, and he must be perceptive enough to keep his feet in a morass of trickery and despair. He must also have learned to deal with intensive attention; other children are ignored at times by their parents, but with the schizophrenic every move and word is taken personally. As a consequence he must become skilled in concealing his emotions, he must learn to indicate that whatever he did just happened and he is not responsible for it, he must perceive the threats in every situation, and he must achieve skill in stabilizing whatever system he is in by being a willing scapegoat to support the inadequacies of those around him. It should be immediately evident that few people can meet the complicated requirements of the world of the average schizophrenic. There is one final requirement which eliminates most contenders. Only certain of the great political and religious leaders of the past have had the character structure, the determination of the schizophrenic. He has the will to devote his life to an absolute and stubborn crusade. His crusade is this: never to let his family off the hook. The hundred million affronts he has suffered are never to be forgiven to the end of his days. Even if the law should force him to separate from his parents, he must continually remind them, by bizarre letters if necessary, that they have driven him mad and he plans to continue in that state. His one risk is cure because if cured this means he has forgiven his family, and the true schizophrenic, his will power forged in the fire of a billion conflicts, will not offer that forgiveness even in the face of the most pitiable pleas. Just as the Crusader tenaciously pursued the Holy Grail over the bodies of the infidels, the true schizophrenic will remain attached to his family at all costs and by any methods so that on their deathbeds his parents still have on their conscience this parental disaster.

The Right Sort of Hospital

Only in the mental hospital can schizophrenia achieve its full flowering. Just as a plant reaches its greatest growth in well manured ground, so does the schizophrenic achieve his full range on the closed wards of mental institutions. Yet oddly enough the first reaction of the schizophrenic to hospitalization is a stout objection. Only when he has been incarcerated for a period of time does he recognize the merit of the establishment. Then he is almost impossible to remove. Nowhere in the world can he find an environment so similar to life at home and yet with opponents so much less skilled than the members of his family.

The average mental hospital has been extensively described in the professional literature. One can summarize these scientific reports by saying that the outstanding feature of a mental institution is a kind of formless, bizarre despair overlaid with a veneer of glossy hope and good intentions concealing a power struggle to the death between patients and staff, coated with a quality of continual confusion. The basic art of schizophrenia lies in a genius for dealing with power struggles, and of course in a mental hospital the problem of power is central. It should not be thought that the struggle between patient and staff is unequal. True, the staff has drugs, tubs, cold packs, shock teatments (both insulin and electric), brain operations, isolation cells, control of food and all privileges, and the ability to form in gangs composed of aides, nurses, social workers, psychologists and psychiatrists. The schizophrenic lacks all these appurtenances of power, including the use of gang tactics since he is essentially a loner, but he has his manner and his words and a stout and determined heart. He also has had extensive training in a family made up of the most difficult people in the world. A normal person might disintegrate or capitulate on any issue in the face of the organized assault by the staff of a mental hospital, but the schizophrenic at one glance can size up the situation and seize upon his opportunities. Even though disconcerted by being betrayed into the hospital, as he usually is, the schizophrenic can have family and staff embroiled in an argument before he has been stripped of his civilian clothes and had his money and driver's license confiscated.

The first lesson the schizophrenic learns in the hospital is that he must do what the aides tell him to do. His initial reaction is to decline, since he has never in his life done what he was told, it is against family tradition. However, the aides cannot permit recalcitrance since it is their duty to keep the hospital functioning. Therefore when the schizophrenic refuses to obey an order, the aide hits him as hard as he can in the gut. This astonishes the patient, and he muses over how to turn it to his advantage. He soon learns that he cannot, because being hit in the gut receives no publicity. Should the patient complain, the aide denies that it happens and the doctor pretends to believe him. That night the aide hits the schizophrenic as hard as he can in the gut twice more and calls him a squealer. From that time on the schizophrenic obeys the aide, although his courage is apparent even in these circumstances because he does what he is told in a desultory manner as if he has not heard a command and is only happening to follow it. In more modern and progressive mental hospitals the aides are not allowed to beat up on the patients. It is necessary for the aide to report that the patient cannot control his hostility so that the doctor can bang the patient in the head with a shock machine. This procedure maintains the proprieties for medical investigating boards who know medical treatment when they see it. Recently institutions have attempted to incapacitate the schizophrenic by pouring drugs into him until his eyeballs float and he is uncertain what is up and what down. Drowned in sufficiently powerful drugs, the schizophrenic's keen perception becomes impaired and he is less skillful in the hospital power struggle. However, over time, immunity to the drugs begins to set in, and recently there has been a trend in hospitals to return to the shock machine.

After his first encounter with the brute force of the hospital structure, the wise schizophrenic casts his dull and calculating eye upon the basic game he must play to survive and keep his self respect. He soon learns that little is new; all is like life at home.

The first weakness the schizophrenic discovers in the hospital structure is the same one he found in his family; the hospital can be hoisted on its own pretense of benevolence. Just as the parents defined all they did as done for his sake, so does the hospital define all it does to be for the benefit of the schizophrenic. Arrangements which suited parents' convenience were said to be for the child's best interests, and all hospital activity which is for efficient operation or convenience of the staff, whether forcing patients to rise at six in the morning or cutting out random portions of the brain, must be said to be for the sake of the schizophrenic. It is when he is offered such benevolence that the schizophrenic manifests his most skillful appearance of confusion, disorientation, and delusion. If he is told he must be in bed at nine in the evening because of his need for rest (and not the convenience of the ward staff) the schizophrenic will experience night terrors which keep the ward in turmoil until his more reasonable bedtime. Having forced the hard fist of the aide or the heavy hand of the psychiatrist on the shock machine to quiet him, the schizophrenic has won the acknowledgement that nine o'clock bedtime is a hospital convenience. Hanging a psychiatrist on his benevolence is best illustrated by the patient who was faced with a doctor who could not tolerate his patients milling about the ward indicting him for his inability to cure them. He therefore announced that for their sakes the patients must be out of the ward all day getting fresh air. This particular schizophrenic declined to leave the ward. When he was forced out the front door, he walked straight ahead until he bumped into a tree, remaining there outside the doctor's window with his forehead against the tree until the exasperated physician retrieved him later in the day.

The hospital also provides the schizophrenic with the comfortable feeling he is still at home with his family by the similarity in power structure. Just as mother maintained the pretense that father was in charge, while ignoring him, so does the nurse pretend the ward psychiatrist is in charge while running things herself. The schizophrenic soon finds that the ward psychiatrist is as unavailable as his father ever was, since of course the psychiatrist never has the time or inclination to talk to the patients. The schizophrenic finds too that his long training in stirring conflict between his parents is unusually valuable in the hospital where nurse and psychiatrist can be played off against each other with minimum maneuvers. The confusion between doctor and nurse over their official and actual power position can be touched off in quite simple ways. For example, when the doctor requires some activity of the patient, the schizophrenic can indicate that the nurse said he was not to do that. The doctor may reply that by God he is the one who makes such decisions, but he becomes uncertain in his dealings with the nurse, who feels in turn that she must have antagonized him in some inexplicable way. If necessary to go to extremes because of a dull-witted staff, the patient can begin to scream whenever a particular staff member comes near him, thus making the entire staff look upon that person with suspicion.

The schizophrenic's training in manipulating coalitions across generations comes in appropriately in the hospital. He can join psychiatrist against nurse, nurse against aide, social worker against ward doctor, ward doctor against hospital administrator, staff against family, and so on. More skillful schizophrenics will escape occasionally and join community and police against the hospital. On the rare occasions when the schizophrenic is provided with a psychotherapist, he has the entire confusion in the staff power structure to play upon. The therapist, like mother, can be persuaded to request that the schizophrenic be given special treatment or at least be more fully understood and the ward psychiatrist, like father, will bluster ineffectually that the patient must do what is expected of him, while the nurse protests that despite what the patient implied she wasn't out of her office for two hours leaving the ward unattended, and the aide will say that it's clearly a paranoid delusion when the patient says he was hit in the gut during the night. These periods of excitement alternate with long days of boredom for the schizophrenic, just as at home.

Whenever he is sufficiently bored, the schizophrenic can provoke action to enliven life on the ward. In fact, many schizophrenics have found they can provide some excitement by *not* doing anything. For example, they can stop eating. Just as mother went into a panic at home if her food was ignored and her poor child was wasting away to her shame, so does the hospital staff develop waves of anxiety if the patient ignores their food. Before reaching the point of no return, the schizophrenic will usually begin to eat again. Some clever schizophrenic's will time their resumption of food to coincide with a new drug the doctor has given them. Since the staff is always hoping for a pill which will cure all the staff problems, they rejoice with each success of a new drug — only to discover later that other patients do not respond to it and schizophrenics have duped them again.

The position and function of the schizophrenic in the hospital is identical with his position and function at home. The staff of a mental institution feel themselves to be outcasts in the profession, insignificant wretches incapable of human accomplishment. Therefore it is essential for their survival that they surround themselves with people who are more incompetent than they are. Living among the experts in failure, the schizophrenics, the staff can stand a little higher in the world. From the top administrator of the hospital who kicks his assistant when irritated, down through the hierarchy to the aide who kicks the patient when irritated, the structure requires that final someone that all else can feel superior to — and there we behold the schizophrenic. As at home, the bad feelings and difficulties of the staff members with each other can be excused as a product of dealing with such a difficult person as the schizophrenic, so that his valuable function as a scapegoat binds the entire structure together like an adhesive.

It should not be thought that just anyone, including people with other psychiatric problems, could fulfill the schizophrenic's function. Training, persistence, and ingenuity are required. There is also a need for courage because of the risks. The schizophrenic not only faces the daily possibility of the aides fist and the psychiatrist's shock machine, but he also lives under the threat of total isolation in solitary confinement as well as the threat that the doctors will plunge a scalpel into his brain as a last resort. Because of medical advances, he now lives with a 40% chance that his anti-psychotic drugs will give him irreversible brain damage. These dangers add spice to the schizophrenic's life, and they require a particular style of behavior from him. This style is known medically as symptomatic of the hospitalized person. Since clear rebellion or justifiable outrage against the institution provokes savage punishment for his own good, the schizophrenic must behave like a difficult person while indicating that it's not he who's doing it and besides he cannot help himself—this is the definition of mental illness. The staff is reluctant to give him the business since he cannot help himself and so they must flounder in dealing with him—this is called treatment of the mentally ill. The most basic way to behave in a difficult manner and deny that it is your own fault is to say that you are someone else and so aliases are common among schizophrenics. However, the mere alias is not enough, it should be one which is clearly an alias, such as a male patient calling himself "Miss United States." Alternatively, one can say that the behavior originated elsewhere, and therefore one should not be punished. A nice device to achieve this is to say that a "voice" told one to do it, therefore responsibility lies elsewhere. One can make any criticism of the staff, even accuse a puritanical nurse of unsavory thoughts, if one says that it is really the Lord speaking and one is merely an instrument for that voice. The nurse becomes uncertain about putting the Lord on the shock roster. Another procedure is to act clearly insane so that one is obviously not responsible for needling the staff. A way to do this is to appear to be disoriented in space and time, which is particularly effective if it carries within it an indictment of the staff. To say that the place is really a prison and it is the seventeenth century is to make it clear that one is too insane to be blamed for an act. Yet at the same time the resemblance to a seventeenth century prison is close enough to most hospitals to arouse the guilt feelings of the staff. One thereby can indict while disarming and escaping blame, all neatly in one maneuver. Sometimes the guilt can be aroused by more ironical disorientation; one can say, for example, that the hospital is a palace and the doctor a king, thereby dismaying the doctor with the comparison. A third procedure is to make caustic comments while giving a silly and dilapidated laugh — who can punish such an idiot, and yet the comments simultaneously reach home. One can also indict by actions without ever saying a word. When a schizophrenic stands against the wall with his head hanging down and his arms outstretched, the staff suspects that they are being told that they are crucifying the patient, yet they are told in a way that they cannot accept or deny the accusation, or blame the schizophrenic — here lies the true art of schizophrenia.

These few simple procedures may seem limited, but a skillful schizophrenic can provide tremendous variety in his use of them. Whenever he has finally driven the staff to bring brute force to bear, it could be expected that the staff does so with the guilty feeling that they are taking advantage of a poor, helpless victim who cannot control himself. However, to assume that the staff feels guilty is to underestimate their education. After all, psychiatrists have received a liberal college education, thorough medical training, and a full residency in the science of psychiatry. They are usually good-hearted men attempting to do their best, and they follow civilized rules in dealing with the human being. Because of their education and knowledge of the history of men, they are able to use a device which has always been used by civilized men caught in a death struggle for power with other men — they define the other men as not human beings, and therefore anything goes. The good-hearted Southerner can give the Negro his lumps and the good-hearted concentration camp guard in Germany can fling people into the gas chambers as long as he can define those people as subhuman. Knowledge of this tradition has helped the psychiatrist to define the schizophrenic as not a person but a thing, an organic hulk who is out of contact with reality. Therefore civilized rules do not apply. By adopting this point of view and building it into a theory of psychosis, the staff can agree that the patient is not responsible for the trouble he is causing because he is not really a person and therefore brain damaging drugs are obviously necessary to point the beast in a more amiable direction. Only by arguing that civilized rules do not apply to the schizophrenic can the staff meet the patient on at least equal terms, because the schizophrenic too is unwilling to follow civilized rules. Driven by his terrifying despair, he will go to any extremity of self-abasement and therefore has a great advantage in such a struggle. The staff is faced with a person of extraordinary determination and skill in innovations. Even stripped nude and flung into a cell without furniture and sound-proofed so that he cannot be heard, the schizophrenic is still not incapacitated. Ordinary people who must rely on friends, furniture to fling, or at least insults when they are in a power struggle would collapse in futile hopelessness in such a situation. Yet locked up alone and unheard, the schizophrenic still finds ways to express his opinion of the staff and arouse them further. He is willing to use the products of his own body and he will pee upon the door and crap upon the floor, cheerfully drawing pictures of the staff upon the wall in what he considers appropriate material.

Since there is some variety in the hospital environment, from reasonably pleasant wards for showing visiting dignitaries to the miserable back wards ruled by sadistic nurses and aides, it is important that the patient learn how to deal with the staff so that he forces them to behave badly to him but only if he has arranged it. He does not mind misery that he has provoked, but he does not like people to treat him badly on their own initiative. Therefore the schizophrenic must do a diagnosis of the staff to find the areas which are most suitable for provocations. The staff too must have an estimate of the range of skill of the schizophrenic so they can know what maneuvers to expect of any individual patient in this struggle. The need for a quick estimate of the schizophrenic has produced psychologists who are willing to do psychological testing so that the staff can diagnose the patient's weak points and thereby gain an advantage in dealing with him. Schizophrenics, however, are not put off as normal people would be by the aroma of pseudo science exuding from the pores of the psychologist. The patients see immediately that this fellow who sits down pleasantly with them and asks them to look at blots of ink and talk about them is indeed a man who does not have their best interests at heart. In fact the schizophrenic knows what he says about the ink blot will be held against him and affect his career in the hospital in ways he cannot predict. Therefore the wise schizophrenic is guarded in his comments about the ink blots. Faced with the same kind of ambiguous situation he was raised in at home, with equally disastrous effects if he should say the wrong thing, the schizophrenic will avoid describing any coherent picture, because he knows this staff member may make ulterior use of the coherence. Instead he will point out little pieces of the ink blot here and there and make no connections between them. He will also avoid mentioning any of the human shapes he sees, even if they look like the psychologist, because he cannot be sure whether the human beings in power over him will take his comments personally. The more self-confident schizophrenic will toy with the test, reaching for bizarre points to see if he can shake the deadpan expression from the psychologist's face, playing with the idea of a bat since he is supposed to be bats, and occasionally making oblique references to violence to indicate that he knows that this threat lies behind the testing. Only indirectly will he indicate that looking at blots of ink seems rather silly and so he knows there must be some reason for it which is being kept from him. The psychologist is pleased with the schizophrenic's protocol because he can discover that the responses are not common, ignoring the fact that the situation of the schizophrenic is also rather uncommon. It is like the white man in the South who concluded that a Negro was ignorant because the fellow shuffled and scratched his head and said, "Yassah, Boss," ignoring the context which made it wise for the Negro to behave in that way. Since psychologists have a trained incapacity to examine contexts, they write down in their reports that the patient is confused and loose in his associations, has distorted perception, deeply repressed hostility, and a sprained ego. This scientific description of test results is given to the staff, which uses it, as the schizophrenic knew they would, to determine where to place him and how to deal with him.

It would seem evident that schizophrenia can be a dangerous

game, but it has its lighter side too. Occasionally, for example, the patient is given a chance to have psychotherapy. Although the ward psychiatrists are so flooded with patients they do not have time to talk with them, and would hardly know what to talk with them about if they did take the time, most hospitals report in their publicity brochures that they are not merely prisons because they have a therapy program. This consists of group therapy meetings led by social workers. It is the function of these meetings to (a) turn the schizophrenics upon each other so they will be less occupied with entrapping the staff (this is called the Keseyan function); and (b) provide the social workers with a feeling of being useful while also letting them vent upon the patients the feelings they have developed from attempting to deal with the patient's families. The schizophrenic usually uses these group meetings to sharpen and broaden his techniques of verbal comment. Often he uses them to practice subtle variations in his repetitious behavior; the schizophrenic is, of course, the master at repeating the same behavior until the staff is driven to distraction. A possible record is held by the schizophrenic who, in a period of only two years, said, "I think my thinking is not good," a total of two hundred million seventy three times.

Occasionally a hospital will have a psychiatrist training program, and here the schizophrenic might have an opportunity for individual psychotherapy with a resident. The profession considers it wise to start these young fellows out on schizophrenics so that anything they meet later when making their fortunes in private practice will be anticlimactic. Psychiatric residents are a peculiar lot. Either they chose psychiatry because they thought they were going mad and it might help, or they could not develop a passion for some other medical speciality, like proctology, and so they fell into psychiatry by default. Once in training they discover that little of what their teachers say is of any use to them in dealing with a schizophrenic. The instructors teach only part time and make their living in private practice where they entirely avoid schizophrenics (having had enough of them when they were residents). The basic problem of the resident is one of translation.

His instructors talk in one bizarre language and the patients in another. While the instructors talk about dark Ids flooded with anxiety and the daffodil structure of ego syntonics, the schizophrenics talk about the influence of atomic energy upon the burontonic systems and the difference between he-cocks and she-cocks. It is forbidden for instructors or residents to talk directly about the central theme of hospital life, the power struggle among staff and patients.

A typical beginning interchange between patient and psychotherapist can be presented to illustrate the kind of skill required of the true schizophrenic. The patient is brought to a room by an aide who mumbles something about seeing a doctor and then shuffles away. The schizophrenic waits, uncertain what new tactic the staff is offering, and attempting to estimate its degree of savagery. At this point the door opens and a vacant-faced young man enters. He wears a suit and tie to distinguish him from the patients. "Hello," he says with a false heartiness, "I'm Dr. Offgamay." The schizophrenic stares at the wall as if he has not noticed the intrusion. "Well," says the doctor, attempting to ignore being ignored, "I thought we might talk about things." This typical therapeutic gambit, the vague, ambiguous, open-ended statement interests the patient. It may even arouse his admiration since it is a degree of ambiguity he thought only his parents could achieve. He begins to test whether this man is really what he appears to be or is more dangerous by saying something like, "My taillight is on," or perhaps, "My head was bashed in last night."

"Well now," says the young man, uncertain what to do with that sort of statement, "I'd like to know a little bit more about you, won't you tell me about yourself."

The schizophrenic, who knows perfectly well his record has been carefully examined for his history, has already understood the situation and he decides on a further test for confirmation. He says, "I want to do what you do."

The doctor freezes — his status position shaken by this mild remark as if by an earthquake. "Oh," he says, his voice rather cool, "how long have you been a *patient* here?"

The schizophrenic has finished his testing, and he replies, "I was born here." He makes this statement with absolute sincerity, as if he fully believes it. "Born here?" says the doctor, so confused by the sincerity that he can only inquire, "How old are you?"

"A hundred and eighty-seven," says the schizophrenic. The doctor suddenly has that lost feeling of one who suspects he is being put on and has been provoked into making a fool of himself and yet cannot be sure. The result is continuing suppressed fury and desperation as the game goes on and the doctor finds himself constantly provoked into saying what he would rather not say. He can only grab onto his shaky status position as a passenger holds the door handle on a wild ride down a mountain road.

This illustration of a typical interchange demonstrates the quick perception and interpersonal skill of the schizophrenic. If they had competitions, schizophrenics would vie among themselves to see who could discover most quickly whether he was dealing with a worthy opponent.

Once the therapy is off to this fine start, the only skill required of the schizophrenic is to keep it going. After all, the therapist is usually the only one in the hospital who will speak to him, except for the aides, who have more muscle than wit. The schizophrenic must keep the therapy ongoing by not creating too much fear and despair in the therapist while at the same time not allowing anything which might approach success. Since residents change every few months, it is also good to give an impression of being almost cured so this resident can encourage one of the next crop of residents to continue the treatment. Some schizophrenics can achieve strings of eight to ten psychotherapists over time, each one feeling that he is almost able to "reach" this poor wretch and a few more interviews will bring about a breakthrough.

The skill of the schizophrenic comes into play in several ways in psychotherapy. He must provide stimulation for the therapist and keep him coming, but he must also provide sufficient exasperating difficulties to help the therapist feel that he faces a worthy challenge of his abilities. Keeping the therapist on the hook requires an avoidance of any direct confrontation of the therapist with his miserable incompetence, as part of a courtesy procedure. For example, if the therapist is late to an appointment and does not bother to apologize, it is not correct to directly confront him with his rudeness or he is likely to flee, as mother did when directly confronted with her misbehavior. Rather, the schizophrenic must tell a story which allows the therapist to correct himself if he chooses. For example, the patient can say. "I was out on my submarine this morning, and we were to meet the refueling ship off Madagascar, but unfortunately the ship had been struck by an atomic bomb and barely limped in late with its Chinese flagons at halfmast." This rather complex statement, which any schizophrenic can quickly devise, allows the therapist an out. He can say, "I'm sorry I was late today." or he can argue, "Now Sam, you know you weren't out on a submarine this morning, you were right here in the hospital." The therapist's recognition that there might be more here than meets the vacant eye is usually represented by his following such an argument with, "Now let's try to get an understanding of why you'd think you were on a submarine. What does a submarine mean to you?"

A further requirement of the schizophrenic is an ability to find out quickly what the current psychiatric ideology is so that he can provide the young therapist with support for the theories he is learning. If it is a period where genital symbolism is the order of the day, the patient must discuss kings being overthrown and virgin queens married and vaguely rub his crotch whenever he mentions his mother. If genital symbolism is out and oral symbolism is being emphasized in training, the patient must quickly adapt to oral metaphors. He will discuss the cement in his stomach and the whiteness of milk, he can offer drawings which vaguely resemble breasts to the keen psychiatric eye, and he may make occasional sucking motions with his lips to stimulate the therapist. The skillful schizophrenic can read the interests of therapists from minimal cues, such as lighting up of the eyes when some obvious symbol that makes sense in theory is mentioned. The more Sullivanian fads require more skill from the patient. As the therapist struggles to handle his interpersonal defenses and to help the patient discover how he deals with people, the patient must offer interpersonal behavior which is easily enough interpreted by even a novice therapist. For example, he must fold his arms and cross his legs and turn his head away so the therapist can point out that he is building a wall between them and interfering with their interpersonal relationship. However, the patient must not merely help the therapist, he also must occasionally show the novice that he still has a great deal to learn. When the young fellow is feeling rather confident in his therapeutic acumen, the schizophrenic can stare thoughtfully at him and then look away and say, "There are some people in the world who have a homosexual fix." Such a comment will shatter any sensitive resident and leave him dragging through the day wondering about his unconscious desires.

The odds against a schizophrenic in a hospital meeting a skillful therapist of schizophrenics are so great that in the memory of those who keep track of these matters the last time it occurred was in Buffalo in 1947. Should this happen, the full range of schizophrenic genius is necessary. He must play therapist against staff, make a thrust at every weak point in the man, pretend improvement when there is none, and generally fight for his life. After all, if he is inadvertently cured he must go out of the hospital to the family waiting for him at the gate. That family has discovered their child can be the burden which holds the family together while still being in the hospital with a hired staff to deal with the inconvenience, and so they protest how welcome he is without wishing him back. The occasional families who actually wish the patient to return home have marshalled their forces in his absence and plan to make up for lost time in giving him the business. Should the patient go mad and become normal, he also faces a society which will blacklist him for having accepted hospital treatment.

Psychiatry today is going through revolutionary changes, and we owe to the schizophrenic many of the advances being made. It is evident that the schizophrenic is responsible for the recent movement to close down all mental hospitals. The leaders of this movement, the more prominent psychiatrists in the field, have suggested that rest homes should be created for the aged and emergency wards be set up in general hospitals for people to stay for a few days during family crises. Mental hospitals would be discarded with a state law that psychotic patients could not be kept in custody more than a few days unless they had committed a crime. The proponents of this scheme argue that schizophrenics should be returned to the families who deserve them and psychiatrists should be forced to deal with the insane and not just drug them and avoid them.

Enthusiasts for the mental hospital, a group composed of families of patients, psychiatrists in peaceful private practice, and those people employed in such institutions, argue that such a radical change is fantastic. These patients are diseased and need medical care, they say, and besides they don't make sufficient income to pay psychiatrists for treatment. The moral wing of this faction also point out that it would be unfair to loose psychotics upon the profession of psychiatry. Just as one would not put a man who runs the mile in four hours in the same race with a man who runs it in four minutes, so it is unfair to face the average psychiatrist with a schizophrenic or his family.

However, enthusiasts for closing down the hospitals argue in turn that such an act is necessary because of the skills of the true schizophrenic. As one proponent put it, "When patients were confined at home, it was thought they would improve with hospital treatment. Now let us admit defeat. Despite all attempts at reform and promising new methods of approach, the schizophrenic has beaten us. We should concede that fact and find other ways to deal with him." More active advocates of closing down mental institutions have created a slogan which can be seen on the signs they carry as they picket mental hospitals, "Let's get the patients off the back wards and back home into the back rooms!"

THE ART OF
BEING A FAILURE
AS A THERAPIST

What has been lacking in the field of therapy is a theory of failure. Many clinicians have merely assumed that any psychotherapist could fail if he wished. However, recent studies of the outcome of therapy indicate that spontaneous improvement of patients is far more extensive than was previously realized. There is a consistent finding that between fifty and sixty percent of patients on waiting list control groups not only do not wish treatment after the waiting list period but have really recovered from their emotional problems—despite the previous theories which did not consider this possible. Assuming that these findings hold up in further studies, a therapist who is incompetent and does no more than sit in silence and scratch himself will have at least a fifty percent success rate with his patients. How then can a therapist be a failure?

The problem is not a hopeless one. We might merely accept the fact that a therapist will succeed with half his patients and do what we can to provide a theory which will help him fail consistently with the other half. However, we could also risk being more adventurous. Trends in the field suggest the problem can be approached in a deeper way by devising procedures for keeping those patients from improving who would ordinarily spontaneously do so. Obviously merely doing nothing will not achieve this end. We must create a program with the proper ideological framework and provide systematic training over a period of years if we expect a therapist to fail consistently.

An outline will be offered here of a series of steps to increase the chance of failure of any therapist. This presentation is not meant to be comprehensive, but it includes the major factors which experience in the field has shown to be essential and which can be put into practice even by therapists who are not specially talented.

1. The central pathway to failure is based upon a nucleus of ideas which, if used in combination, make success as a failure almost inevitable.

Step A: Insist that the problem which brings the patient into therapy is not important. Dismiss it as merely a "symptom" and shift the conversation elsewhere. In this way a therapist will never have to examine what is really distressing a patient.

Step B: Refuse to treat the presenting problem directly. Offer some rationale, such as the idea that symptoms have "roots," to avoid treating the problem the patient is paying his money to recover from. In this way the odds increase that the patient will not recover, and future generations of therapists can remain ignorant of the specific skills needed to get people over their problems.

Step C: Insist that if the presenting problem is relieved, something worse will develop. This myth makes it proper not to know what to do about symptoms and will even encourage patients to cooperate by developing a fear of recovery.

Given these three steps, it seems obvious that any psychotherapist will be incapacitated whatever his natural talent. He will not take seriously the problem the patient brings, he will not try to change that, and he will fear that successful relief of the problem is disastrous.

One might think that this nucleus of ideas alone would make any therapist a failure, but the wiser heads in the field have recognized that other steps are necessary.

2. It is particularly important to confuse diagnosis and therapy. A therapist can sound expert and be scientific without ever risking a success with treatment if he uses a diagnostic language which makes it impossible for him to think of therapeutic operations. For example, one can say that a patient is passive-aggressive, or that he has deep seated dependency needs, or that he has a weak ego, or that he is impulse ridden. No therapeutic interventions can be formulated with this kind of language. For more examples of how to phrase a diagnosis so that a therapist is incapacitated, the reader is referred to *The American Psychiatric Association Diagnostic Manual*.

3. Put the emphasis upon a single method of treatment, no matter how diverse the problems which enter the office. Patients who won't behave properly according to the method should be defined as untreatable and abandoned. Once a single method has proven consistently ineffective, it should never be given up. Those people who attempt variations must be sharply condemned as improperly trained and ignorant of the true nature of the human personality and its disorders. If necessary, a person who attempts variations can be called a latent layman.

4. Have no theory, or an ambiguous and untestable one, of what a therapist should do to bring about therapeutic change. However, make it clear that it is untherapeutic to give a patient directives for changing — he might follow them and change. Just imply that change spontaneously happens when therapists and patients behave according to the proper forms. As part of the general confusion that is necessary, it is helpful to define therapy as a procedure for finding out what is wrong with a person and how he got that way. With that emphasis, ideas about what to do to bring about change will not develop in an unpredictable manner. One should also insist that change be defined as a shift of something in the interior of a patient so that it remains outside the range of observation and so is uninvestigable. With the focus upon the "underlying disorder" (which should be sharply distinguished from the "overlying disorder"), questions about the unsavory aspects of the relationship between therapist and patient need not arise, nor is it necessary to include important people, such as the patients' intimates, in the question of change.

Should student therapists who are not yet properly trained insist upon some instruction about how to cause change, and if a frown about their unresolved problems does not quiet them, it might be necessary to offer some sort of ambiguous and general idea which is untestable. One can say, for example, that the therapeutic job is to bring the unconscious into consciousness. In this way the therapy task is defined as transforming a hypothetical entity into another hypothetical entity and so there is no possibility that precision in therapeutic technique might develop. Part of this approach requires helping the patient "see" things about himself, particularly in relation to past traumas, and this involves no risk of change. The fundamental rule is to emphasize "insight" and "affect expression" to student therapists as causes of change so they can feel something is happening in the session without hazarding success. If some of the advanced students insist on more high class technical knowledge about therapy, a cloudy discussion of "working through the transference" is useful. This not only provides young therapists with an intellectual catharsis, but they can make transference interpretations and so have something to do.

5. Insist that only years of therapy will really change a patient.

This step brings us to more specific things to do about those patients who might spontaneously recover while in treatment. If they can be persuaded that they have not really recovered but have merely fled into health, it is possible to help them back to ill health by holding them in long term treatment. (One can always claim that only long term treatment can really cure a patient so that he will never ever have a problem the remainder of his life.) Fortunately the field of therapy has no theory of overdosage, and so a skillful therapist can keep a patient from improving for as long as ten years without protest from his colleagues, no matter how jealous. Those therapists who try for twenty years should be congratulated on their courage but thought of as foolhardy unless they live in New York.

6. As a further step to restrain patients who might spontaneously improve, it is important to offer dire warnings about the fragile nature of people and insist they might suffer psychotic breaks or turn to drink if they improve. When "underlying pathology" becomes the most common term in every clinic and consulting room, everyone will avoid taking action to help patients recover and patients will even restrain themselves if they begin to make it on their own. Long term treatment can then crystallize them into therapeutic failures. If patients seem to improve even in long term therapy, they can be distracted from improvement by being put into group therapy.

7. As a further step to restrain patients who might spontaneously improve, the therapist should focus upon the patient's past.

8. As yet another step with that aim, the therapist should interpret what is most unsavory about the patient to arouse his guilt so that he will remain in treatment to resolve the guilt.

9. Perhaps the most important rule is to ignore the real world that patients live in and publicize the vital importance of infancy, inner dynamics, and fantasy life. This will effectively prevent either therapists or patients from attempting to make changes in their families, friends, schools, neighborhoods, or treatment milieus. Naturally they cannot recover if their situation does not change, and so one guarantees failure while being paid to listen to interesting fantasies. Talking about dreams is a good way to pass the time, and so is experimenting with responses to different kinds of pills.

10. Avoid the poor because they will insist upon results and cannot be distracted with insightful conversations. Also avoid the schizophrenic unless he is well drugged and securely locked up in a psychiatric penitentiary. If a therapist deals with a schizophrenic at the interface of family and society, both therapist and patient risk recovery.

11. A continuing refusal to define the goals of therapy is essential. If a therapist sets goals, someone is likely to raise a question whether they have been achieved. At that point the idea of evaluating results arises in its most virulent form. If it becomes necessary to define a goal, the phrasing should be unclear, ambiguous and so esoteric that anyone who thinks about determining if the goal has been achieved will lose heart and turn to a less confused field of endeavor, like existentialism.

12. Finally, it cannot be emphasized enough that it is absolutely necessary to avoid evaluating the results of therapy. If outcome is examined, there is a natural tendency for people not fully trained to discard approaches which are not effective and to elaborate those which are. Only by keeping results a mystery and avoiding any systematic follow up of patients can one insure that

therapeutic technique will not improve and the writings of the past will not be questioned. To be human is to err, and inevitably a few deviant individuals in the profession will attempt evaluation studies. They should be promptly condemned and their character questioned. Such people should be called superficial in their understanding of what therapy really is, oversimple in their emphasis upon symptoms rather than depth personality problems, and artificial in their approach to human life. Routinely they should be eliminated from respectable institutions and cut off from research funds. As a last resort they can be put in psychoanalytic treatment or be shot.

This program of twelve steps to failure — sometimes called the daily dozen of the clinical field — is obviously not beyond the skill of the average well trained psychotherapist. Nor would putting this program more fully into action require any major changes in the clinical ideology or practice taught in our better universities. The program would be helped if there was a positive term to describe it, and the word "dynamic" is recommended because it has a swinging sound which should appeal to the younger generation. The program could be called therapy which expresses the basic principles of *Dynamic Psychiatry, Dynamic Psychology*, and *Dynamic Social Work*. On the wall of every institute training therapists there can be a motto known as *The Five B's Which Guarantee Dynamic Failure*:

> Be passive
> Be inactive
> Be reflective
> Be silent
> Beware.

IN DEFENSE
OF PSYCHOANALYSIS

Skill in prophecy was not distributed equally among the population, and so perhaps some of us might be forgiven for not anticipating that psychoanalysis would be missed in so short a time after its death in 1957. Who could have suspected that in only a quarter of a century after its demise there would be mourning in the clinical arena for what has been lost. Many of us were simply blind to the assets of psychoanalytic ideology and training. As we look at psychiatry today, and the clinical professions generally, anyone can see that the trend, like water going over the falls, is downward. Let us review the past merits of psychoanalysis from the current mainstream perspective.

Curiously, the actions of the psychoanalyst which were most opposed are now the ones most missed. For example, it was objected that the analyst erred by not doing anything. Opposing any active intervention into a patient's life, the psychoanalyst handbook proclaimed, "We must listen. All other action except active listening is proscribed, except there can be an occasional interpretation if there is no danger that the interpretation will in any way be manipulative or a direct influence toward change."

As we examine that position from today's view, at once we note its chief merit—it kept the clinician from harming anyone. On the blackboard the Professor of Psychoanalysis wrote *Rule Number 1*, "Physician do no harm," and so required the young analyst to do as little as possible to avoid that eventuality. If he erred and did harm, it took so long that corrective mechanisms occurred in the life of the patient. As we look at the actions of psychiatrists today, it is as if that rule, and that blackboard, have spun off into a Szasian black hole in space.

To be more systematic, let us examine a series of factors which were once objected to by the anti-psychoanalytic movement and see what has been lost to the field.

Training

The classic objection to psychoanalytic training was that it took so long there were only grey heads in consulting rooms. By the time he was given his analytic credential, the eyesight of the analyst was too poor to read it. Such jokes reflected the dismay felt by many people because of the long and expensive training in irrelevancies. Despite Freud's wishes, his followers decided that psychoanalysis should be a medical specialty, and so being in the club required long medical training before anything relevant to psychodynamics was taught. (Towards the end, in the period of degeneration and desperate search for candidates, psychoanalytic institutes opened up to psychologists and other laymen, but that was a deviation from the original design.)

Looking about today and seeing what has happened, there were obvious advantages in requiring candidates to be medical doctors. Granting that nothing psychologically relevant is learned in medical school, and analysts never practiced medicine, still there were important benefits. First of all, it limited the profession to people intelligent enough to pass examinations in medical school. The task might not require brilliance, but it eliminated from practice people with I.Q.s under 80, in contrast to some of the other therapeutic professions today. As part of medical training, the analyst was also required to spend several years as a resident on the wards of psychiatric hospitals. This experience was his first introduction to psychoanalytic ideology because there was a rule that all heads of psychiatry departments had to be psychoanalysts. That was once thought to be unfortunate because those department heads concealed from psychiatric residents the fact that there were 102 schools of therapy existing out in the world. Only the limited psychodynamic view was taught. Yet today concealment is even more severe. The heads of psychiatry departments now must be psychiatric-biologists who do not even know that therapy is done out in the world, and so they cannot help keeping a knowledge of therapy from residents. In many psychiatry departments, therapy is an elective, available to a resident only as a curiosity if he has time after studying the main subject, the arsenal of chemical restraints imposed in practice. Some departments forbid therapy being discussed, so that just as residents in psychoanalytic departments once secretly attended seminars on family therapy, now residents attend secret meetings on therapy. The psychoanalytic department heads of three decades ago, despite their obvious biases and narrow views, seem wise and broadminded men whose absence is sorely missed in psychiatry today.

After medical school and residency, the analyst attended the psychoanalytic institute where he had years of seminars and suffered a training analysis. Freud suggested that a few months of analysis might help a youth learn his, or her, biases. By the time psychoanalysis died, the training analysis was averaging 7 years. Can one imagine in the world today anyone speaking a monologue about herself, or himself, several days a week for years and years and years and years and years? Oh, the nostalgia one feels for that time when life was leisurely and an individual thought he, or she, was that important.

What was the chief merit of requiring medical school, residency, and years at the institute? Anyone can see at once that the primary purpose was to allow the young analyst to grow older and have life experiences before being turned loose on the public. Contrasting that lengthy training with what is required today is like contrasting graduate school with kindergarten. Psychiatrists now come from accelerated medical programs that can be pass-fail, there are brief psychiatric residencies in the use of drugs, and a psychiatrist can be out practicing while almost a juvenile. For other professions, the age is even younger: it is possible to be licensed by the State as a proficient therapist when hardly out of college. The social worker with a B.A. spends a year or 2 in social work school learning about the history of social work and then can be legitimately out in practice. Psychologists grow older in laboratory research, the only merit of that long training for a therapist, but they do not achieve half the age of the psycho-analyst. Today new species of therapists with odd degrees are

licensed. Some are called marriage therapists, some family therapists, some Christian ministers, and some socio-educational-
psychologists. With a one year Master's Degree they are released
upon the public unacquainted personally with marriage or children, except as peers. The quick training is clearly irresponsible
when contrasted with the psychoanalyst who devoted his youth
to becoming accredited and his old age to increasing the requirements for accreditation for the next generation.

It would be silly, of course, to say that growing older was
the only merit of the long psychoanalytic training. After all, the
training years were filled with doing something. Typically the
years were spent becoming acquainted with the bizarre kind of
people who deserve treatment. The young analyst learned to
classify a great variety of patients and give them their proper
names. The importance of this training is evident when one sees
young therapists today who fumble with the pronunciations in
the DSM III Diagnostic Manual and generally find themselves
puzzled by strange people. Of course, for the psychoanalyst the
chief value of recognizing and categorizing patients in training
was to be able to identify these patients he, or she, would eliminate from private practice. This skill, known as the Landean
Principle, makes it possible to have a quiet private practice with
the kind of people who behave themselves, never provide an
inconvenience, and expect little or nothing.

In contrast, many young therapists today do not discover
unusual types of people until they are surprised by them in the
office where they have the responsibility to cure them. Social
workers are taught little about abnormal psychology, and psychologists are largely taught the psychology of rats, which is
appropriate for only some of their human clients. Yet both professions learn more about psychopathology than many of the
marriage and family therapists who have not been in mental
hospitals or mental health clinics, as professionals, and so never
observed the varieties of problem people. In contrast, any psychoanalyst was not only taught to recognize the mentally ill, but she,
or he, had teachers devoted to showing ways to avoid them.

Non-Directiveness

Granting that aging and learning to diagnose were important psychoanalytic contributions, there was also the insistence that a therapist should be non-directive. However, only the naive would think that this was because analysts did not know how to give directives. The Gregory Bateson award for the *Skillful Use of Power in Therapy* must be given to the group which directed thousands of people to lie on their backs and talk to the ceiling while their analysts sat out of sight behind them. To successfully direct so many people to behave so bizarrely for so many years, and to pay so much money to do it, is an incredible accomplishment.

In relation to non-directiveness, the most important contribution of psychoanalysis was the definition of the social role of the professional. Here we miss them most. If we examine the dedication of the analyst to the non-directive stance, we see at once that it leads to a posture quite different from today's therapists. Because the psychoanalyst took no action and gave no directives, he found himself respecting the individual and avoiding any manipulation or influence. "Let us reason together," was the only intervention of the psychoanalyst. Whatever mad ideas or unfortunate plans the patient offered, the analyst discussed them with him and sought the roots in the depths of his unfortunate mind and his childhood miseries.

Psychoanalysts were accused of having a theory that only awful things are inside men and women because of their concern and preoccupation with an unconscious mind full of hostile and aggressive drives and conflicts. However, one forgets that they respected the right of the individual to his awfulness. Typically the patient chose to continue with the symptoms after the analyst had explored their meaning and origin in a successful analysis, but it was the free choice of the individual to continue to be miserable. When asked advice by a patient, the analyst would, of course, offer none, saying the person must make up her, or his, own mind about everything. Never giving advice, the analyst also never directed anyone into any new activity nor deliberately responded with reinforcements to encourage a preferred way of behaving. Such actions would have required the analyst to decide what was the preferred behavior for a person, and he did not wish to impose life goals upon his clientele. He only wished to induce a patient into a strange psychodynamic world view for thinking about these goals.

If we contrast this benign tolerance with what is happening today, we see therapists pushing their clients around in the most arrogant manner. Without clear understanding of the person or his situation, young therapists not only advise clients and direct them, but they paradox them and trick them out of symptoms indirectly. Generally they do not mind saying how a patient should live, or saying the person should not be depressed or have psychological symptoms, and they will require people to fit their views of normality. No analyst would have imposed his views in that way. As therapy techniques become more powerful, wisdom becomes more necessary. We look back nostalgically on the kindly analyst who would simply say, "You must make your own decision about whether to blow your brains out, but I will miss you if you do."

The Family Opponent

The inability of the psychoanalyst to deal with families was thought to be a deficit, but looking back, that also had its merits. Taught to be the advocate of whatever family member came to him, the analyst would refuse to talk to any other members of the family. That extreme posture seemed silly at the time, but what is our perspective now? Granting that not involving the family directly usually prevents change, still that is only one aspect of the issue. Getting involved with whole families can cause a therapist to thrash about helplessly with them and end up going along with what he, or she, would rather not because of family pressure. Avoiding the family prevents this kind of participation. There are also civil rights issues. Not all parents are kind, and when parents take action to harm a child, or each other, the victim finds himself, or herself, in the hands of a therapist. If that person is an analyst, an expert is immediately on her, or his, side. "I stand against the whole family network," was the analytic posture. Such a posture can freeze the family system in pathology, but it also places outside authority upon the side of a victim. Certainly the analyst could not be used as an agent of parents or social workers who wished to institutionalize a difficult offspring because the family was upset.

Similarly, social service workers enjoy yanking children out of homes to rescue them from neglect or abuse. Such unconcern with the ultimate destiny of the child, and of the parents, and lack of interest in what might be done to improve the parenting in the family, is improper and naive. If the child had been to an analyst, no one could persuade *that* expert to take any action to put the child anywhere. Instead, the analyst would reflect with whoever came to see him about what the person wished to do, think, and understand. Not being an advocate of social action, the analyst could not be used to participate unwisely in such action.

Schizophrenia

It is when we turn to schizophrenia that we most clearly realize how we miss the psychoanalyst. Perhaps a way to express this complex subject is to illustrate it with an anecdote about what happened on a television talk show. There were several psychiatrists, including one psychoanalyst, discussing mental illness. The psychiatrists represented different schools, but all of them enunciated the psychiatric party line that schizophrenics have a physiological defect and should be drugged, no matter how brain-damaging the drugs. "Schizophrenia is a brain disease," announced one of the psychiatrists. "Of course it is a brain disease, everyone knows that," said another. "Not everyone," said a third, who was a family psychiatrist, "because there is no actual evidence of any brain disease, and no one has won the Nobel prize for finding such evidence." The other psychiatrists began to shout in anger, and this man quickly said, "But I agree, even in the absence of evidence, that brain disease is probable as the basis of psychosis." He added, attempting to make a joke, "I'm not a Dopamine." But humor was not allowed. "Not probable, it *is*, it *is*, it *is*, it *is* brain disease," cried the other psychiatrists in unison.

When the psychoanalyst obtained the moderator's attention, he said, "I am not too sure about all this. I knew a woman and everyone said she was schizophrenic and had brain disease, but I talked with her and it seemed apparent to me that she had a fixation on her father. She was obsessed with him, and I think that was the root of her behavior and her psychosis had a child-hood origin."

"No, no," shouted the four psychiatrists, "if she was a psy-chotic it was brain disease, brain disease, brain disease!"

"But . . . ," said the psychoanalyst.

"Brain disease, brain disease," they all shouted, and they pounded on the table until the psychoanalyst subsided.

In this scientific debate, clearly the psychoanalyst was a humanist interested in a person, which made him seem like a creature from the stone age in that psychiatric group. We look back nostalgically to that golden time before anti-psychotic medi-cations when kindly psychoanalysts had their influence and of-fered a humanistic view even on the wards of psychiatric hospitals.

If we puzzle over why the psychoanalyst thought of the schizophrenic as a human being, there is one obvious explana-tion. We must remember that analysts were trained many years ago before psychotic people were routinely medicated into a state of zombydom. Schizophrenics were always the great teachers of psychiatric residents. The first experience of residents doing therapy was with schizophrenics even though they would avoid them in practice after graduation. Schizophrenics have the knowl-edge and skill to help make a psychiatrist human. Intensively struggling with a psychotic, the young psychiatrist becomes more humble and more wise as schizophrenics easily find his weaknesses and guide him to self-discovery. Young residents can become arrogant, realizing their social power, and they learned humility by being undone by a schizophrenic. Everyone knows the true nature of man is learned from men who are mad.

What has happened now? The young psychiatric resident today has never met a schizophrenic who was not drugged into being dull-witted. Recently a young patient said to his therapist, "I would like to blow up the world." The therapist, a psychiatric resident, panicked and called for drugs and custody, fearful of a malpractice suit if there was an explosion. Obviously the resident had never been trained by a drug-free schizophrenic. Incapacitated by drugs, schizophrenics no longer function as effective teachers and the profession suffers. How else can we explain the fact that psychiatric residents of this generation are not as wise as those of several generations back? Not only is every schizophrenic immediately medicated at the hospital door, but if any mental patient on a ward shows any imagination or intelligence he is immediately diagnosed psychotic with brain disease and drugged.

As we see psychoanalysis fading, like a watercolor painting left too long in the sun, we notice that analysts are most sorely missed because of this plague of drugs in psychiatry. Taking what they concede is "The Big Gamble" today, psychiatry is hoping against hope that they will find something biologically wrong as the cause of mental illness. If they find it, they will be leaders in the field because mental illness will be an illness, with evidence, like diabetes. That will give them the right to drug all deviants in the population into insensibility. What makes the gamble exciting is that if they don't find a biological cause, as they have not, they will be outcasts in the clinical field and humanists will throw rocks at them. At the moment the most they can do is shout, "Brain disease, brain disease," and increase their dosages of powerful medications to persuade everyone that they must have discovered a physical cause or they would not be doing so much harm. It is now the rule that some psychiatrist must appear in

Time magazine once a month saying that a breakthrough is about to occur in finding the biological cause of schizophrenia. After many years of such publicity, it is not surprising that many people have the impression that surely a biological cause must exist. The campaign keeps the research funds rolling in, supporting the psychiatric and drug laboratories.

As part of the gamble, there is also a present payoff. Psychiatrists have always faced the problem that they could only treat one patient per hour and so were limited in their potential income. All other physicians had the payoff of several patients per hour. The new generation of psychiatrists, however, has found a way to do as well as other physicians. By having P&P sessions, known by that name because they consist of pushing pills, a psychiatrist can see from four to six patients an hour with medication interviews and so make four to six times as much fees. Actually, the more innovative psychiatrists have been using compliant social workers to persuade a patient's family that the patient is incurable and must always be on medication. This preliminary interview, known as the Andersonville Ploy, makes it possible for a psychiatrist to waste less time on a patient with persuasion, and so he can see even more patients per hour in medication interviews.

Another accusation against psychoanalysts was that they were accused of seeing patients for years. Now psychiatry has the benefit of a theory that patients must always stay on medication and so the patients can be seen, and pay, forever.

The gamble that psychiatry is taking would only be good fun if it were not for the fact that anti-psychotic medication causes brain damage, and vast numbers of people are having their brains scrambled each day. Tardive Dyskinesia, a type of neurological damage which is irreversible in half the cases, is spreading like a plague across psychiatry-land. Thousands and thousands of people now shiver and shake and helplessly bite their tongues and grimace like idiots. This uncontrollable behavior is a psychiatry induced malady called Psychiatric Parkinsonia caused by P&P sessions. Unpredictable in its onset, the disease appears when anti-psychotic medications are given and then withdrawn. When the psychiatrist sees the Parkinsonian reaction when the drug is withdrawn, he immediately re-institutes it to conceal the misfortune. That stops the symptoms but increases the brain damage so that later more unfortunate symptoms appear. The gamble is that later, when the symptoms are revealed to be a national disaster, a biological cause will have been found for mental illness and that will excuse the biological damage of vast numbers of people. The more daring and experimental psychiatrists are now giving brain damage to 8 year old children, if they can find any reason to call them autistic and so not human. Meanwhile, out of guilt, an increasing number of psychiatrists are having nightmares where they are pursued by vast numbers of their fellow men who are grimacing and shaking and mumbling epithets. These unfortunates do not even have psychoanalysts to help them understand these nightmares.

To illustrate a special way psychoanalysts are missed, let us contrast the statements of a contemporary psychiatrist on the subject of anti-psychotic medication with those of a psychoanalyst. Any psychiatrist is now taught always to medicate; the issue is only which drug to choose. He is also taught to defend the consequences of the medication. First, he must say that he is puzzled by these rumors of Tardive Dyskinesia because he has never seen it (this is sometimes called Frank's ploy). He also learns to insist that powerful medications for psychosis and depression only cause brain damage because (a) the wrong dosage was used and (b) it is only if people are on medication for 71 years, and those who get brain damage from being on it only a week have something wrong with them, and (c) anyone who has Tardive Dyskinesia should not be bitter and sue his psychiatrist because he should prefer it to psychosis, and (d) besides drugs have to be used because for two generations no psychiatrist has learned how to treat the mentally ill except by drugging them, and (e) besides, the patient's family insist on drugs to keep him at home and behaving himself and how could a psychiatrist be expected to oppose a mother and father? It should be noted that many of these arguments were developed by an earlier generation of psychiatrists because they are essentially the ones used to defend lobotomies.

What is the psychoanalytic posture in this controversy? It is simple — drugs are not to be used in treatment. How we miss that elementary wisdom today. Analysts would not drug patients even if parents were on the threshold of forming consumer groups to have them lynched. (Perhaps occasionally a deviant analyst in a private psychiatric hospital used drugs, but it was with proper guilt and shame.) How can the human mind be explored when in a fog of powerful medications? The psychoanalyst was also properly trained so he knew how to talk to patients about other matters besides the effects on them of their medication, unlike the current generation of psychiatrists who can only sit helplessly fondling their syringes if unable to medicate.

As we look back nostalgically, the psychoanalyst appears on the horizon in the setting sun in increasingly attractive colors. He was a man who was mature when his training was complete; he was familiar with a whole range of human problems as a diagnostician; and he was an advocate of the patient's rights against the family, the court, and colleagues. He was a student who had been taught by medication-free schizophrenics, and he was against the use of damaging chemicals in treatment. Where are such men and women now that we need them? If only psychoanalysts had known how to change anyone, or even relieve a symptom, they would still be a major force in the clinical field and would be exerting their benign influence for all of us to this day.

TOWARDS A RATIONALIZATION FOR DIRECTIVE THERAPY

Among the mysteries of therapy is how so many intelligent people can reach such different conclusions about what therapy is and how it is to be done. The differences among the many schools of therapy are not minor, they are disagreements about fundamental assumptions. One can choose almost any issue and find differences.

What is the purpose of therapy? Some therapists say it is to change a person with symptoms and normal people do not need it. Other therapists say therapy is to help people grow and expand and normal people or anyone else will benefit from it.

What is the responsibility of the therapist? Some say it is the therapist's responsibility to bring about a change and he, or she, must know how to do so. Failure is the fault of the therapist. Other therapists believe their only responsibility is to join the client in a human encounter, if not a mystical communion, and help him understand himself: whether the client changes is up to him, or her. Some therapists even consider it improper to try to change someone deliberately.

What is the cause of change? There are two extremes. Some therapists believe that change occurs only through insight and self understanding and so they explore with clients hypotheses about their nature. In contrast, other therapists believe that change is caused by a shift in a person's behavior and social situation and insight is irrelevant. In a single clinic there may be cognitive therapists attempting to change a person's ideas, thoughts and feelings by focusing on them directly. In the next room the opposite is happening: a therapist is directing changes in a person's behavior and relationships on the assumption that ideas, thoughts and feelings only change when behavior changes. How can such differences exist among people in the same field dealing with the same kind of problems? One might almost suspect that the human mind has different compartments which do not communicate well with each other, and therapists are representing and focusing on different parts.

Therapy seems to have developed originally to deal with a special class of people. These are people who behave in deviant ways and say they cannot help themselves. Often they are puzzled as to why they do what they do. Some are compelled to act in certain ways, others avoid acting in certain ways, others are depressed and cannot act at all. Some cannot eat and others cannot stop eating. There are those who cannot go in an enclosed space, others cannot go out in an open space. What they have in common is that they say their behavior is beyond their control. Often they say they know they are being irrational. It is as if the part of their minds which explains what they do is independent of, or even disconnected from, the actions they take.

To explain the behavior of people who are irrational, one approach has been to postulate that people have essentially two minds. One is rational and reasonable. But the "other" mind is not logical; it follows irrational ideas and associations. There is a rational, conscious mind divided from the irrational unconscious.

It is possible that the idea of the "unconscious" developed out of observations by hypnotists at the end of the last century. A hypnotist would suggest to a subject that after he awakened he would go over to the door and touch the doorknob three times. The subject would do that. When asked why he did it, the subject did not say, "Because the hypnotist told me to." Instead, he came up with reasons which seemed irrational because they were not part of the hypnotic context. For example, he said, "I have to touch brass at regular intervals, and the doorknob is made of brass." Or he said, "I just wanted to feel something round in my hand at this time." Unaware that he had been told to do the act, the subject sought a reason, no matter how irrational.

A unitary theory of the mind could not explain such contradictory behavior. Therefore it was postulated that there must be a part of the mind that is outside the awareness of the conscious mind. That was called the unconscious, and it was argued that this part of the mind was not only outside awareness but accepted illogical rationalizations.

At the time there was a division of schools of the unconscious: one group proposed that the unconscious contained unfortunate ideas and conflicts, which was the Freudian position. Another school argued that the unconscious was a positive force which would act in the person's best interest, which was the position of hypnotists represented by Milton H. Erickson. But both groups defined it as outside conscious awareness.

The idea of two parts of the mind became important in therapy. It was decided that irrational behavior could be cured if a person examined the ideas in his unconscious mind with his conscious mind and found the meaning behind them. All would be rational again if the irrational was explained. For example, the conscious mind would discover that avoiding touching some object was actually a rational act if one accepted the irrational idea in the unconscious that touching was related to sex. The premise in this therapy orientation was that the discovery of the irrational notions behind behavior could cause change.

With the postulation of the conscious/unconscious mind, it was assumed that the explaining part of the mind controlled behavior. An elaborate set of procedures based on this idea was developed by Sigmund Freud, who argued that man was driven by his unconscious ideas but he could influence them. That was a major focus of therapy until the 1950s, when therapy began to change and the premises adopted were not merely different but the opposite of what had gone before.

The two new major theories of therapy which developed were the ideas of behavior therapy based on learning theory, and the ideas of family therapy based on the systems ideas of cybernetics. Both of these therapeutic approaches seemed to simply set aside the issue of the mind, conscious or unconscious. Instead of accepting the argument that people behave as they do because of their thinking processes, most behavior therapists and family therapists assume that the way a person thinks is a result of the way he behaves. The behaviorists focus upon changing the reinforcements the person is responding to when behaving in deviant ways. The family therapist sets out to change the sequences in the family that elicit a deviant response from the person. It is argued that a person is driven to behave as he does by the behavior of other people rather than by his unconscious mind.

The question of the thinking process is largely bypassed in these approaches. The emphasis has been on communication. If a person is forced to respond to multiple levels of conflicting communication, as in double binds, he will behave deviantly. He will then rationalize his behavior to try to explain it. It is assumed that if his communication situation becomes "normal," his behavior will become normal, and his thinking will become rational. That is, it is assumed that the rational part of the mind does not govern behavior, but that when behavior changes a changed rationalization is required.

The shift in therapeutic procedures based on these premises has been remarkable. Formerly a therapist sat with an individual client and encouraged the client to talk, occasionally making an insightful comment. The task was to change the person's thinking, ideas, and emotions. The therapist was expected to be a wise philosopher who could listen, understand, and provide a human encounter as well as wisdom about life. In contrast, the new therapies assume that a therapist's responsibility is to bring about change by directing the person into new behavior and organizing a new set of responses among his intimates. The therapist does not talk about the meaning of life, except as a way of joining the person, but requires new sequences of behavior induced by straightforward and paradoxical directives.

Not only is it assumed that the ideas in the mind change as a consequence of changes in behavior, but it has begun to be assumed that memories also change. Just as amnesia can be arranged with hypnosis so can it occur naturally as a result of the therapeutic relationship. People talk about their pasts differently when their current behavior changes. So the therapist can change the person's past as well as his present (and future).

From the behavior view, "unconscious dynamics" and reported childhood experiences are a rationale provided by a person for explaining his behavior, but not necessarily a "truth" about the past. As behavior changes, the rationale changes; therefore the past is different. Sometimes this effect is marked. For example, it was noted that if a brief therapy intervention relieved a symptom, afterwards the person might think of the symptom as always having been minor. That is, a person with incapacitating headaches would say after they disappeared, "Oh, yes, I used to have headaches," in a way that made them seem trivial. The past had changed.

It could be argued that a therapist changing the present is not changing the past but merely changing the person's memory of the past — that there is a true past but that it can be remembered differently. That is possible, but it is also possible that what is true about the past is changeable and changing memories changes the past. In that case to dwell on the miseries of the past, as in focusing at length on how abused this person was as a child, can change the past to one where the primary experience was abuse, when that might not have been so before the therapy.

As new, more social therapies developed, no theory of the mind evolved to accompany them. Obviously the idea that people behave in response to reason was inappropriate with the new views. It was also largely irrelevant whether ideas were within or outside the person's awareness. In the absence of a new theory, the nature of the mind seems to have been simply neglected by the new therapeutic approaches. Perhaps this is why the therapists of these schools were sometimes accused of being shallow or even anti-intellectual. But what is needed for this stage of therapy is a different model of the human mind; one that is appropriate to the new strategies for change and for dealing with the complex social network. The concept of unitary mind is not sufficient when there appears to be behavior outside awareness. The conscious/unconscious division of the mind, or the left brain/right brain division, does not seem complex enough to account for systematic behavior among people. It has been estimated, based on the examination of slow motion films of body movement and linguistic analysis, that two people in a conversation exchange 100,000 bits of information a minute. Obviously a simple dichotomy of conscious and unconscious is not sufficient to deal with such complexity. I recall Gregory Bateson objecting to the concept of the conscious/unconscious mind by suggesting that he was not puzzled why there was an unconscious mind, but why there would be a conscious mind. How could one be conscious of all the complexity of human social interchange?

To make sense of the new complexities, as well as various kinds of illogical behavior, it seems we need a conceptual model which assumes the mind has a number of parts and even assumes that these parts tend to respond independently of one another and independent of rational thinking and explanation. Fortunately, perhaps in response to social changes, a new model of the brain is developing which postulates more complexity. Research on the brain is suggesting that it is composed of a number of modules with different functions. One module specializes in offering rationalizations, or explanations, of why the organism behaves as it does.

Let me quote Gazzaniga in his recent book, *The Social Brain**: ". . . the human brain has a modular-type organization. By modularity I mean that the brain is organized into relatively independent functioning units that work in parallel. These relatively independent modular units can actually discharge and produce real behaviors . . . our species has a special brain component I will call the 'interpreter.' Even though a behavior produced by one of these modules can be expressed at any time during our waking hours, this special interpreter accommodates and instantly constructs a theory to explain why the behavior occurred. This special capacity . . . is a brain component found in the left dominant hemisphere of right handed humans." And he adds, " . . . we seem to be endowed with an endless capacity

---

*Gazzaniga, Michael S., *The Social Brain*, New York, Basic Books, 1985. pp 4, 5.

to generate hypotheses as to why we engage in any behavior."

Examining this way of thinking about the brain, even from an oversimplified view, or even using it as a metaphor, this possible model of the brain answers many questions not answered by a simple division of the brain into two parts. If we assume different areas of the brain have different functions and that they operate somewhat independently of each other, at times there will be conflicting behavior. The module that rationalizes the person's behavior will have to offer an explanation that is illogical if the behavior it is trying to explain is illogical and conflicting. Therefore at times people will offer an irrational description of their behavior.

If the rationalizing part of the mind has little influence over behavior but only tries to make sense of it, the implications for therapy are profound. There are also answers to a number of questions. This modular view of the mind makes it seem reasonable that a person can have habitual symptomatic behavior and be puzzled why that is so. The rationalizing part of the mind observes the behavior and the person's response is, "I cannot help myself." The person will act and be puzzled, or he will make up hypotheses to try to make sense of the action.

The behavior of a person with symptoms and the behavior of a hypnotic subject are essentially similar in this regard. In each situation the behavior is "involuntary" in the sense that the person denies responsibility for the action. At one time, because of this similarity, hypnotic subjects were used to demonstrate symptoms. With hypnotic directives one can induce phobic behavior, compulsions, amnesia, and the various types of "involuntary" psychopathology. For both symptoms and hypnotic behavior, the disassociation process makes more sense with this model of the mind. If one part of the brain organizes behavior in response to directives, and the interpretive part of the mind can only explain what is happening and has little direct influence on the behavior, the hypnotic subject or the symptomatic patient will be compelled to act and will be unable to explain why.

It is in the use of hypnosis in therapy that one observes most sharply the division between the mind's rationalizing module and the behavioral modules. Typically the hypnotist not only directs certain behavior but often distracts the rationalizing part of the mind so it will not interfere. It is like tricking the interpretive module so that its hypothesis making activity will not interfere with what is happening. As a typical example, Milton H. Erickson reports the case of a man who was afraid to go up in an elevator in high buildings. He was hypnotized and directed to focus on the sensations in the soles of his feet while going to a particular address. His only attention was on the foot sensations. He followed the directive, and of course the address was up in a high building and he had ridden an elevator to get there while preoccupied with the sensations in the soles of his feet. From then on he could go up in high buildings. The interpreting part of his mind had been distracted from the new behavior.

Another way of distracting the rationalizing part of the mind is to induce amnesia. For example, with a good hypnotic subject one can say something like, "Today is Tuesday, but it might be . . . " and in that pause give various hypnotic directives. Then the hypnotist can continue the sentence by saying, " . . . Wednesday or even Thursday." The subject will have amnesia for what happened in the middle of the sentence. The mind seems to continue a rational continuity by completing the sentence and therefore must drop out of awareness what happened in the middle of it.

Spontaneous amnesia could occur if the rationalization module is compelled to explain behavior and at times that behavior is unexplainable; a way to respond would be to simply forget it. Much of hypnosis is rather like anaesthetizing the left brain, or rationalizing part of the mind, and giving directives to other modules. It might be possible to map the brain by hypnotic experimentation, just as one might explain experimental results in hypnosis by the new map of the brain being developed.

A number of therapists have noted that insight, or understanding what is behind a symptom, occurs after a therapeutic change, not before. This concept of the brain would make sense of that. A behavioral change would force the brain to attempt to rationalize the new behavior. It would come up with explanations that integrate the past and present. To explain why a symptom was no longer bothersome, it would also be reasonable to minimize the previous distress of a symptom.

When we examine the development of a symptom, it seems possible that the hypotheses that have been created are only speculations. For example, it was assumed that a phobia was a product of a past traumatic event. The person afraid of dogs was assumed to have once been bitten by a dog. There was even a therapeutic theory that recalling the memory of the event would make the phobia go away, and so there was a tendency to create such an event. Now the evidence is accumulating that a person with a phobia may never have experienced a past event that caused it. We lack longitudinal studies which give evidence of how people were before they developed a symptom and how that behavior came about. We can only speculate. But it seems possible that one of the modules of the brain, independent of conscious choice, could organize and develop symptomatic behavior. As Gazzaniga puts it, "These modules can compute, remember, feel emotion and act. They exist in such a way that they need not be in touch with the natural language and cognitive systems underlying private conscious experience."*

The failure and interminable length of insight therapy can be explained if one assumes the rationalizing module of the brain has little influence on behavior but creatively makes hypotheses to explain it. A therapy devoted to exploring the mind and examining hypotheses about behavior would be unsuccessful but popular with intellectuals. Because of the complexity and ingenuity of the brain, an explorer of creative hypothesis would be occupied for many years and always find new aspects of the mind to explore. It should be noted that therapy was created by intellectuals and taught by academicians who believe that knowledge and self awareness are the most important aspect of life. (If one

*Op. cit. p. 86.

trains uneducated therapists, the intellectual bias becomes immediately apparent.) However, if one is setting out to change someone, a therapy devoted to exploring the mind would not achieve that end according to this model.

It is in the field of therapy that the module map of the brain becomes most interesting. It is not merely that it explains various puzzles and mysteries, but it opens up new ways to innovate therapy techniques. Obviously with this theory the idea of directive therapy makes the most sense.

From this view, to change people it is necessary to arrange that they behave differently. This might be done in relation to the therapist, or the intimates of a client might be organized so they respond differently and thereby compel a different response. As the behavior changes, the mental and emotional processes change because the behavioral modules of the mind are influencing the mental processes. Obviously, from this view the strategies of directive therapy would be the treatment of choice.

Granting that change occurs when new behavior is required, it seems possible to influence the rational mind to change by using directive interventions. It would seem that two ways of influencing the mind have had effects which, if they do not change behavior, at least disrupt the person's pattern of thinking so that directive interventions are more acceptable. These two ways are introducing paradox, and introducing the absurd. To adapt to a paradox, the thinking process must change. For example, when a client is accepted in therapy to be changed and then is directed to stay the way he is, there is no logical way to rationalize that. Such a paradox occurs in many forms, from encouraging a symptom to restraining a client from changing. In my experience, the paradox needs to be followed by implicit or explicit directives for change if change is to occur.

Another way to influence the rational mind is to introduce the absurd. A therapist can offer ideas and interventions which are random or relevant to some totally different context. To rationalize such absurd interventions, the thinking process must change, and the client then seems to be more open to direct interventions.

It is interesting that hypnotic trance can be said to utilize both paradox and the absurd. Hypnosis is in itself paradoxical insofar as the subject is directed to behave spontaneously. The subject is asked to behave in a certain way and also to indicate that he is not deliberately doing that.* Similarly, the subject is sometimes asked to respond to an absurd directive, such as seeing himself with three arms. It would seem the rationalizing part of the brain responds to paradox and absurdity by separating itself from the behavior, making the behavior more amenable to change.

There does not seem to be a framework in Western philosophy for a therapy theory leading to paradoxical and absurd interventions to induce change. However, there are the practices of Zen Buddhism, which also seem to lack a theory of the mind. To break people out of over-intellectual thinking and focus them on the present rather than the abstract, the Masters pose paradoxical questions and make absurd interventions (while not allowing trance behavior as a response). Many of us who developed a directive, non-intellectual therapy drew ideas and support from that age old Buddhist practice.

As the model of the brain changes, what are the changes in the ethical issues of therapy? The idea of informed consent for a therapeutic procedure is based on the assumption that the client's rational mind should judge and approve what is to be done. Therefore to avoid consulting the client's rational mind, or to trick that mind so change occurs outside awareness, might be considered unethical. Yet if the rational mind has the least influence on behavior, should its judgments be accepted? If its hypothesis generation potential allows it to find many reasons to continue distressing behavior, then should that part of the mind not be distracted so that directives can bring change.

A model of the brain which defines the interpretive part of the mind as following after behavior is of particular ethical interest in relation to long term, insight therapy. If cognitive and

*cf. Haley, Jay, *Strategies of Psychotherapy*, New York, Grune and Stratton, 1963.

insight therapy focus upon the rationalizing, interpreting part of the mind, they are dealing with the part which has the least influence and so should have the poorest outcome. Is it ethical to take money from a client to do therapy with the procedure that has the least effect?

In summary, in the last few decades we have seen therapy change from a thoughtful and insightful consultation with a wise philosopher to an active process of telling people what to do in direct and subtle ways. Those of us who preferred a therapy that tells people what to do and focused upon the real world in the present were often on the defensive over the years, even if the therapy had the best outcome. We were told by philosopher therapists that we were manipulative, naive, and not sufficiently deep. We could not fabricate a theory of the mind which supported what we found in practice to be the most successful therapeutic approach. Now we find that the trend in brain research which postulates a more complex brain supports the argument for a more simple, directive therapy.

HOW TO HAVE AN AWFUL MARRIAGE

Everywhere there are articles, books and professional therapists offering advice on how to improve and save marriages. What is missing is a guide to how to make a marriage miserable. Granting that some people enjoy marriage, what of the vast numbers of marital couples who seek an unhappy marriage, as they must or they would not quarrel so much and give so little pleasure to each other. Determined to be miserable, these people have nowhere to turn for advice. Often they divorce and marry again and again. Each marriage is a search to find one more awful than the last, when if they had stayed with the first spouse and had a little instruction they could have found sufficient misery there.

Despite all the literature on how to have a happy marriage, only recently has anything been written on how to have one that is unhappy. Fortunately an anonymous author has just completed an in-depth study on how to produce marital misery, whether the marriage is heterosexual, homosexual, or mysterious. Now the primary text in the field, this scientific work is of encyclopedic size and called, *Achieving Misery in Two Group Dyads with Special Emphasis on Married Couples*. Unfortunately it is as tedious to read as it is to suffer the marriage failures it describes. For the interested public, a summary is offered here of the ways to achieve an awful marriage.

We can skip over the history of marriage in that opus and get right to the instructions on how to make marriage miserable. The history only emphasizes that marriage is of such a nature that an outside force has always been necessary to force married couples to stay together. First the church made harsh laws against separation and divorce, and later the state took over the job of making divorce difficult. Now, with the abdication of the church and the freedom given by the state, anyone can divorce at will. The expanding divorce rate is the inevitable result. If one sets out to have a miserable marriage now, there is a risk of separation which did not exist in the past. The ease of divorce has led to a change in the basic marital threat. The spouse who can threaten to leave the other has the most power in a marriage because the other will capitulate in fear of separation. However, now with separation so easily possible, that threat to flee the marriage has become a risky one. Spouses must go after each other with the knowledge that a divorce is easily available. If they miscalculate and escalate quarrels, they risk the possibility that they could separate and the next marriage might be enjoyable.

It is said that anyone can have a happy marriage but people must make their own marital disharmony. That is not quite true. Many people lack the skills to make a marriage awful, and they don't understand the natural development of marriage well enough to take advantage of it. Opportunities for marital misery will be presented here in terms of developmental stages: how to begin a marriage badly, how to make a marriage worse in the early years, what to quarrel about when the children are no longer available, and how to increase marital distress in old age even when strength is failing.

Planning an Unhappy Marriage

One must work at marriage, as every authority agrees. Achieving misery requires conscientious effort. However, the task is surprisingly easy if one can begin badly. There are two general ways to start a marriage so that misery becomes inevitable: one is to marry for the wrong reasons, and the other is to marry the wrong person. Starting a marriage badly is like building a proper foundation for a house: unhappiness is built into the structure from the beginning.

The most popular wrong reason to get married is to flee into matrimony as a way of avoiding something else. A mate for a lifetime is chosen impulsively to get out of a bad situation. There are many situations to escape from: one can marry to get out of poverty, to avoid going to school, to not have to work for a living, and so on. The most common wrong reason to marry is to escape from one's family. If parents are constantly nagging about keeping a room clean so that pestilence will not become a plague, or about coming home in time to get some sleep, or to give up excessive use of drink and dope, then obviously an escape from that repressive atmosphere is in order. If only one can find a young man, or a woman, to marry and share expenses, then freedom comes with one's own apartment. Fleeing home is estimated to be the reason for 81% of the marriages which are awful when spouses are under 21 years of age. "Free at last, free at last," cry the young people as they rush off to their own domiciles. From that point on they hope never to clean house, to stay out all night, to drink and use drugs until they fall down, and generally to enjoy liberation.

Unfortunately, when the only purpose of marriage is to get away from one's family, the marriage itself has no purpose. There is no basis for enjoying each other as a married couple when the selection was not made for that reason. Even someone limited in intelligence can achieve a miserable marriage in this way. Not having selected a mate for compatibility, in a matter of weeks the couple cannot stand each other. They begin to quarrel over who should keep the house clean, who did or did not come home at a reasonable hour, and the drink and dope bring forth meanness instead of joy. Once this situation is structured, very little effort is required by the young people to achieve marital misery. If particularly determined to enjoy distress, they can add pregnancy as a reason to marry and leave the family. Parents will even encourage marriage when they see a baby enlarging a daughter's figure. The addition of a baby to the young couple's sanctuary is like meringue on the pie: opportunities to be miserable increase. The baby can make a worse mess than the young couple alone, it can keep them up later than parties, and generally the child encourages a suppressed fury at being helplessly tied down by this creature they must care for. Endless quarrels are manufactured over whose turn it is to do what for the baby, who should deal with the community protective service agencies when they are accused of neglect, and whose fault it was they had the baby in the first place. Loud arguments about how great life would be if they had not been trapped will announce to the neighbors that here is a couple skillful at making each other miserable.

Choosing the Wrong Person

Almost equal to the opportunities which arise by marrying for the wrong reasons is choosing the wrong person to marry. How does one know how to choose a mate in order to have an awful marriage? The answer is simple; complex psychological tests for incompatibility are not required. It is also not necessary to make a gross error in choice, such as choosing a person of the wrong race, or wrong religion, or wrong class, although such choices lay the groundwork for inevitable trouble and so have their merits. Basically the selection of a person to marry must be based upon two criteria: he or she must have attractive faults different from one's own, and there must be a determination to reform that person and get rid of those faults. Examples can be found just by glancing in your neighborhood in any direction. The classical pair, which is often used as a model in pre-marital misery counseling, consists of the overly responsible woman who is attracted to a man whose faults are that he is too irresponsible and carefree. She admires his self confidence, his willingness to lead the good life, and his entertaining ways. Her faults have always been that she is too shy and responsible and cannot let herself go. The man chooses her on the basis of the same criteria: and he hopes it will correct his tendency to be off the wall, since he wants to settle down. Once married, the couple should proceed at once to reform each other. She must insist he get a better job with longer hours, think about a less pleasant career, not drink so much, stop partying all the time, and save money. He can yell at her to stop counting every penny, enjoy an evening out occasionally, and not be so dreadfully dull. Although this arrangement seems simple, any couple — even one of limited imagination — can use it to make each other miserable for many, many years. Ingenuity is not required, only persistence.

The reverse gender arrangement is also classical in opportunities. The woman who is active and domineering in her career and social life is attracted to a mousy, quiet fellow whose faults are that he is too shy and lacks self confidence. He, in turn, is attracted to her because she has all the spirit he lacks, and he hopes it will rub off on him. Once married, the two people immediately try to reform each other. It is evident that marital misery is easily achieved with that contract. She needs only call him a wimp at regular intervals, while he subtly lets her down to get even with her. By behaving like a wimp, he implies she is an impossibly domineering woman. It is estimated by the eminent Dr. Schiff that at any moment during the day there are 111,200 couples in the offices of marriage counselors with a wife saying she wants the counselor to make her wimp of a husband into a romantic and interesting man to save their marriage.

Variations on this theme are as obvious as pigeons to bird-watchers, but one more common type can be specified. This type of pair is called the Engineer's Syndrome since it is commonly observed among couples where the husband is in the electronics industry. In this arrangement, a wife chooses a husband whose faults are opposite hers. He is logical, precise, rational, and quite unemotional (except in extreme circumstances when his computer breaks down. Then he might become so disconsolate he must be hospitalized.) She is affectionate, emotional, capable of immediate crying spells, and she has a tendency to scream and yell during any discussion of a controversial issue, like the way she keeps house. She, of course, is chosen by the man because he seeks someone who can express an emotion to stimulate that tendency in himself. The outcome is inevitable: as the marital disagreements occur, the wife goes wild and yells. He withdraws, saying, "Why can't a woman be rational and reasonable?" With very little effort on the part of either one of them she can spend her life weeping while he is out working on his sports car, constantly improving something that can be improved.

These ways of beginning a marriage—marrying for the wrong reason and choosing the wrong person—are the most simple ways to assure marital distress. If a couple has a better beginning, more ingenuity is required to make the marriage a misfortune.

Problems of Intimacy and Outimacy

There are two basic areas which can be exploited to the fullest in any marriage: how to make love and how to fight. The best beginning for sexual problems is in the early years of marriage; if well nurtured the problems can continue for many years to come (or years of not coming). The variations on this theme are many, and most couples are capable of all of them. Everyone has heard poor, uneducated people protesting, "Oh, if I only had the education that man has, I could make my wife as miserable as he makes his." That is naive. In the task of creating marital misery, everyone has a fair chance. There is no discrimination on the basis of race, class, or intelligence, as anyone can see simply by strolling about the city and overhearing the action in the houses in different kinds of neighborhoods. The only difference is that one can overhear the misery better in the poor neighborhoods because there are more people and the houses are more flimsy.

The sexual arena offers such opportunity for marital distress that often the marriage hardly begins before the partners decide it is better not to have sexual relations at all, at least with the spouse. The crucial factor for bringing about sexual problems is timing. Sexual arousal and release is a complex physiological and psychological process requiring such timing that interfering with it is not difficult. Generally the rule is to initiate sex at the wrong time, in the wrong place, with the wrong frequency, in the wrong way. The novice chooses one of these wrongs. The expert insures success by managing to use all of them over the course of a marriage. A husband who is the model for us all will always want sex when his wife is not interested or is occupied with something else, he will want it on the living room rug at noon when the kids are coming home for lunch, he will want it every third hour through the night, and he will want it in a position where they can both watch television at the same time. Protests by the wife meet angry accusations that she is frigid. The wife who is an equal match for such a husband will offer equally powerful techniques. She can be totally indifferent, and she can also arouse him and immediately lose interest. At another time she can yell at him and demand more sex at once, protesting angrily if he has difficulty with immediate compliance. If accused of inconsistency, she can say it is before, after or during her period.

A basic rule for sexual problems used by many couples over the years is to not tell the spouse what one likes or does not like in sex, and then to blame the spouse for not being pleasing. A wife who can only achieve orgasm in a certain way should avoid telling her husband that, and throughout the marriage she can be frustrated and pretend orgasms. The husband who prefers to see his wife nude should politely turn out all the lights so as not to embarrass her. Variations on this simple theme of avoidance are obvious and range from avoiding discussions to avoiding each other. If one mate watches TV late and the other goes to bed early, which is the habitual pattern of most couples, each evening announces sexual avoidance.

Spouses are so vulnerable in relation to sex that bad feelings and quarrels can easily be generated. A combination of sexual frustration and righteous indignation is a winning duo. The righteous indignation is best produced by the couple protecting each other. If the husband is uncertain about his potency, the wife can insist she is unable to enjoy sex and so take the blame for sexual avoidance. Instead of appreciating her sacrifice, the husband will be angry at her for her sexual indifference and feel righteously indignant because he is a deprived husband. The reverse is equally powerful; the husband can protect the wife by approaching her sexually in ways she can rightfully protest. He can also wimpishly emphasize his own inadequacies so the fact that she is cool enough to refrigerate food does not have to be faced. One might think that protecting each other would risk the possibility of kindness and appreciation in return, but that is not the case, as every spouse knows. Like a cancer flourishing in a peach, the protection has a patronizing edge that ripens into successful mutual dissatisfaction.

Every survey shows that most couples achieve the most displeasure in the sexual area, and so techniques for achieving sexual dissatisfactions need not be dwelt on here. Every couple has its own favorite variations and innovations.

Quarrels

Besides problems of intimacy, the opposite problem of difficulties with outimacy is essential if a couple is to have an awful marriage. Fortunately couples have been helped to be experts at quarrels and fights because they were able to observe their parents over the years. However, each new generation likes to make its own contributions, and so much marital time is devoted to developing new innovations in that enterprise. A few standard procedures can be described to help the novice.

Quarrels are nature's way of keeping a marriage alive. Marital misery requires quarreling in such a way that nothing is changed and the quarreling must be repeated again and again. Should an issue be solved, a new issue must be found to quarrel about next time, and most couples do not have the energy or imagination to continually develop new issues. It is better to have a few unresolved problems and belabor those throughout the tedium of the marriage. The two ways to end quarrels so they will occur again and again are at opposite extremes: to withdraw and sulk, or to escalate to violence so the quarrel ends with shock and embarrassment but nothing is resolved.

Outimacy includes quarrels which range from violence through verbal abuse to sulks and silences and withdrawals. The withdrawal is the best way to end an argument so that nothing is changed. If the couple backs off into silence with each quarrel, awful issues can be nurtured and maintained for many years. Ending the withdrawal so that the couple can quarrel again is sometimes a problem. With extreme couples the sulking only ends when they are required to speak because a child breaks a leg, or an earthquake occurs. Many issues can remain unresolved for as long as 42% of their marriage. The record is held by the wife who objected to the way her husband said, "I do," at the wedding ceremony and did not speak to him again throughout the marriage.

Violence is the other extreme way that a couple can keep quarrels going without resolving anything. Sometimes it is thought that only some people can be violent, but that does not seem to be the fact. Even couples who are political pacifists and are kind to animals will hit each other. Of course hitting where it shows can attract attention from the community, so one should use restraint and calculation with violence. It is best to start small, as with a punch on the arm, and steadily increase the blows so that in a matter of months noses are being broken. As with any brutality, proceeding a step at a time is important: each level is explored until the couple is used to it. Then the next level of assault does not seem so large. The couple who has escalated in this way can be surprised when neighbors are shocked by blood and broken bones.

A case may help. Once upon a time there was a Ph.D. Biologist and his M.A. in Mathematics wife who got drunk and fought every Saturday night. Those who think that education might make people less violent should realize that it does not and in fact offers new ways that the proletariat does not have available. For example, such people are experienced as teachers, and this husband would teach boxing to his wife. "Here is a left hook." he would say, and hit her. "Here is a right cross." They could also use their knowledge of anatomy to hit each other where it would hurt most and show least. The wife once hit him in the kidneys with a toaster. Of course in this situation each blames the other for what happens. The wife said her husband was a wimp who turned into a monster with drink. He said she provoked him and was the "out of the blue" type because she claimed he always hit her "out of the blue." Once the husband reported that he decided to give up the addiction to hitting his wife. He vowed he would not be provoked to violence. That Saturday she said something insulting, and he told her he wanted to avoid a quarrel. He went into the other room. She followed him and continued to yell at him, according to his report. He withdrew into the hallway. She pursued him. He went into the bedroom and locked the door. She pounded on the door and yelled. Finally she broke the door down and cursed him. He hit her "out of the blue."

This couple was in therapy, and the therapist insisted that a man should not physically abuse his wife no matter what the provocation. Therefore, if it happened again the wife was to call the police. She did this and it ended the violence, but for an unexpected reason. The wife called the police to complain that her husband was beating her, and a young policeman came to the house. He said, casually, "Well, would you like to file a complaint, lady?" The couple had expected the policeman to be shocked by violence occurring in their expensive neighborhood of educated people. The policeman was so casual, obviously having made a number of visits of this kind in their neighborhood, that the couple was embarrassed because their fighting was not unusual. The snobbish husband was shocked enough to stop hitting his wife, not wanting to be common.

Addiction to drugs, alcohol and other substances make marriage misery easy, if not inevitable. However, these potions should be used only if the spouses are limited in their range of skills. To get drunk habitually will make a marriage unhappy, but rather than lean on that crutch, greater skill should be expected of the average man, or woman. Every spouse is capable of sober psychological abuse if he, or she, really tries.

An example of how a couple almost solved a drinking problem that made their marriage miserable illustrates the risk of going to therapists. A young psychologist was visited by a middle aged couple, and the wife devoted the interview to saying that her husband's drinking problem had ruined their marriage. She spoke of herself as a living martyr to his alcoholism. At one point in the interview the husband said that it was difficult to stop drinking, and his wife should know that because she could not stop smoking. She replied that it was not the same thing at all, and his illness was the ruination of their marriage. He said, "I'll stop drinking if you stop smoking." "Don't be silly," she replied. The alert young therapist pointed out that this was her opportunity. Drink had ruined their lives, and now she had only to stop smoking and he would have to stop drinking. The wife provided a 30 minute lecture on how her husband could not stop drinking, and besides she had given up everything in life for him and now she shouldn't be expected to give up her one pleasure, smoking. The skillful therapist, after prolonged negotiations, persuaded the wife to agree that she would stop smoking if her husband would stop drinking. They left the office, and when they came back the following week he was sober and she was not smoking. There was considerable tension between them. They faced the possibility of a more harmonious marriage. The following week the couple came in and the husband collapsed drunkenly into the chair. The wife lit a cigarette. "What happened?" asked the shocked young psychologist. "I'll tell you," said the husband, slurring his words. "Last week I was driving down the street with my wife and she said, go buy me a pack of cigarettes, and she pointed to a liquor store." They had saved their unhappy marriage by good team work, and the therapist gave them up in despair.

Problems of sex, quarrels, violence, and addictions are devices to be used throughout marital life from the teen age marriage to the abuse from wheel chairs in old age. However, different stages of marriage offer different opportunities to magnify bad feelings.

The Early Stages

As authorities have often said, a married couple must work on their marriage. When a marriage does not begin badly, both partners must put in more effort. Generally the early stage of marriage is the time to quarrel about relatives. Children are not yet available and romantic affairs are yet to come. Letting the in-laws intrude into the marriage and then quarreling about them is the primary way to encourage trouble at this time. Whether to go for holidays to the home of her family or his family can be an effective quarrel. Of course if the parents buy them a house or contribute money, the young couple are obligated to stay nearby and maintain the tensions of extended family relationships inside the marriage. A productive quarrel involves in-law employment. The wife, for example, should insist that her husband take that job in father's business. After that, many of the quarrels between them can be about the ways her father intrudes into their marriage. Any complaint of the husband about his job she can take as a criticism of her family and argue that they could not survive financially if it wasn't for her father saving her incompetent husband.

The triangle with mother-in-law can be used in its classic variations and the wise husband will encourage his mother to guide his wife in how to take care of him, because she knows best. An award was recently given at the Awful Marriage Banquet to an elderly couple who were able to quarrel about a mother-in-law for 42 years. Over 60 years old with their children grown and gone from home, this couple could not live together because the wife's 92 year old mother had thrown the husband out of the house in an argument 12 years previously. Some couples who fear that the mother-in-law problem might not last and they will have to develop something else to quarrel about should welcome the new longevity of parents and be reassured by this example that a lifetime can be devoted to this quarrel.

Children

It is possible to see the progress of a marriage as a series of tests to see if sufficient misery can be gained from this spouse, or is another choice better and so a divorce in order. With the arrival of a child, new opportunities arise for couples who are about to separate because there is not sufficient discontent. One can think of it this way; when a couple meet, they feel they can always stop seeing each other. When engaged, they can think that if it doesn't work out they don't need to get married. On the wedding day, they can think, "Divorce is easy, and if this doesn't go the way I like it I'll split, even if all those people came to the wedding." However, with a child arriving, the couple has new responsibilities which force them to stay together and suffer, and it offers wonderful new ways of quarreling. There is a risk, of course, that a child might improve the marriage. However, the odds are that the birth of a child provides a symphony of new opportunities for the couple to make difficulty with each other. Even the question whether to conceive a child, or to keep it when conceived, is an opportunity for intense quarreling.

There are two standard ways to achieve marital distress at birthing time:

a. The wife can ignore her husband and become totally preoccupied with the offspring within her. When the husband comes home from work, saying, "The most important thing in my life happened to me today," the wife can say, "That's nice dear. Wouldn't you like to feel the baby kick?" Conversely, the husband can behave as if there isn't a child on the way. When the wife comes home from work exhausted in her 9th month of pregnancy, the husband can complain that she is simply not keeping up the house like she used to and is neglecting her duties.

b. While the wife is encouraging the husband to resent the baby, the husband can increase marital misery in a way so common it has been given an anthropological name. At this time the wife is vulnerable because she feels ungainly and awkward and unattractive. The husband should choose that moment to take off and pursue life's pleasures. He can disappear with other women, drink to excess, run out of the house at times when she most needs him, and generally share the birth experience by not being there. As she delivers in Philadelphia, he can be on a bat in Schenectady. This way of sharing labor establishes the ground-work for marital bitterness for many years to come. It shows how a baby can be used to promote marital distress before it can itself speak or cause trouble.

The appearance of the baby's head as it comes out to enjoy the parent's company is a sign of opportunity to come. Obviously the infant who cries constantly and has the croup makes its contribution to marital distress, but is it possible to achieve marital misery even with a happy baby? Thousands of couples can attest to that achievement. Not only does the happy baby give the parents a chance to enjoy it and ignore each other, as well as to quarrel over possession, but the in-laws descend like wolves on the flock and offer a resurgence of opportunity for conflict. The child has miraculously given birth to 4 grandparents, and the early in-law struggles reactivate. Grandparents can be specially helpful if they raise questions not only about the ways to raise a child but also about its paternity.

There are so many ways of quarreling over children that a special type of therapy, child therapy, has been created for it and it would take a 200 page index here just to list the types of fights. Generally they can be grouped into two kinds of quarrels: those where marital fights are expressed in terms of the children, and those where the children are blamed for marital fights.

Using the children to express marriage conflicts is learned easily by most couples. If a wife is in conflict with her husband over the ways he patronizes her as a woman, she can quarrel with him about the rights of their daughter to be equal to boys. Should the husband despair over the ways the wife messes up the house, he can yell how the daughter never cleans her room. The wife who wishes to call her husband dumb can emphasize that the son, who is just like him, should be tested because he might be retarded.

Obviously the possibility of separation will decrease with more children available to blame for marital difficulties. The childless couple must exercise far more restraint. No matter how awful a marriage, a couple can say it is only because they have this difficult child who makes them nervous. Or they can offer the most common excuse for suffering in marriage: "we must survive these quarrels and stay together miserably for these awful creatures."

Affairs

As the children grow and become preoccupied with school or involved in their own search for difficult mates, a couple must find other resources. At this stage an affair becomes one of the best possibilities for encouraging marital distress. Just as a pyramid is solid because it is constructed as a triangle, so can unhappiness be produced in marriage by triangulating with someone in a romantic affair. First of all, let us set aside the affairs which do not disturb a marriage, because many couples stabilize their marriage by outside involvements. The spouse does not object but is merely relieved to have his, or her, partner diverted elsewhere. The existence of the routine mistress or the quiet affair makes quarreling inappropriate.

The goal of succeeding in arousing bitterness in marriage must involve an affair that really upsets the spouse. The affairs are on a continuum from those that cause the least bad feeling to those that cause the most. Generally, affairs can be classified as mean, puzzling, or mythical.

a. *Mean.* The mean affair is with a best friend (or, at an extreme, with a spouse's parent). A valuable employee is also a good candidate if it risks the loss of the business and shakes the family financially. It is the mean affair that sends indignation highest in a marriage. The Affair Award was recently granted to a wife who managed to have affairs with every single one of her husband's best friends, without exception. This left her husband in splendid isolation from friends and growing bitter about life.

A variation of the mean affair is to choose a person who is as the spouse was. A husband chooses the moment when his wife is feeling older and despairing over her age and has an affair with a pretty 20 year old who looks just like she did 20 years previously. Generally, the rule with mean affairs is to think, "Who can I choose that would infuriate my spouse but not to the point of divorce and separation, only to a determination to get even?" When that goal is achieved, the couple is on their way to an awful marriage.

b. *The Puzzling Affair* is one that is most appropriate if one has an overconfident spouse. The plan is to choose to be romantic with something that is so inappropriate it is a mystery choice. For example, a man with a wife who emphasizes fashion and sophistication can have an affair with a fat, tacky, uneducated woman and flaunt her to his wife's friends. A dignified, intellectual wife can choose an affair with an 80 year old man, or a 16 year old motorcyclist boy friend of her daughter. In the extreme case the man can choose a young man to have an affair with. This leaves his wife puzzled over what is wrong with her, or him, that was never noticed in 23 years of marriage.

The merit of the puzzling affair is that it creates bad feeling but also uncertainty so the spouse hesitates, not knowing whether to recommend a mental hospital or offer savage retribution.

c. *The Mythical Affair* is one which makes a marriage miserable without actually having to go through the trouble of bedding another person. The spouse only needs to believe that an affair is happening to achieve the goal. Such an affair is easy to set up once one grasps the principle: it is merely necessary to use subtle behavior — or gross behavior if one has a dumb spouse — to arouse suspicions. An odd response to a phone call, or a phone number left on the kitchen sink, or an unexplained absence after work, or not being where one is supposed to be — all these ways of attempting to conceal a real affair are done but without the actual affair. When confronted, the denials should be too extreme, of course. Mythical affairs of this kind have been known to carry on for years, eroding a marriage like rust over time.

One of the awards given in this area was to a man who returned from a war, and his wife was delighted to see him. She embraced him as they sat down on the couch together. About to make love after not having seen each other for two years, the man said, "Wait. I have a confession to make. When I was away,

I had lunch with a woman." The wife said, "That doesn't matter," and she reached out for him again. Then she paused and said, "If it was only a lunch, why would you confess it to me at a time like this?" A quarrel began which was still continuing 24 years later. He had arranged that she could never give up trying to find out what had happened at that lunch. Of course it was necessary to regularly reinforce her suspicions, which he did through years of marriage and the raising of four children. When her attention flagged, he would leave a woman's name on a piece of paper in his desk at his office, knowing his wife would check his drawers. In the argument that followed each time, the lunch of many years ago would come up to be quarreled about again. Not everyone can make his marriage miserable and push a spouse's buttons with so little effort. This man sets a standard we can all admire. There are, of course, debates in the field whether a mythical affair is as good as an actual affair. Specially skilled spouses can have both: a real affair is concealed by a mythical affair involving wrong suspicions which lead the partner in the wrong direction. An actual affair has the merit that it can be miserable and so the person can have both a miserable marriage and a miserable romantic affair, achieving two misfortunes at once. A classical case was a man who had a wife and children and also a mistress with whom he had a child and who functioned essentially as a second wife. He had two dinners every night, suffering an argument each evening with both women.

Marital Struggles in Old Age

When the children are grown and one is too old for an affair, how is it possible to continue misery in marriage? Just as young people do not believe that old people have sex, they also don't believe they will be able to continue marital misery in old age. They need look only as far as the nearest leisure community to get up their hopes. Any couple married for many years has developed such a range of weapons and has quarreled so habitually that they need only minimum cues to arouse the most bitter feelings. For example, one can observe a young couple shopping in the early days of marriage. The husband chooses something on the shelf and says, "This would be nice. I read in Consumer Reports that it is the best." The wife replies, "I don't think it is a good product, let's not get it and waste our time on something you read about in that silly magazine." The husband says, "It is not a silly magazine, and I will have this, and you won't prevent it, and I'm the one who brings the most money into our house." The wife replies, "I'm sure you think you know best, but I break out in hives if I even have that product in the house, so give it to me and I'll put it back on the shelf." That complex interchange has become rather different by the 42nd year of marriage. The husband says, "This?" and holds up the product. The wife replies, "No!" The man says, "Yes!" The wife takes it from his hand and puts it back on the shelf. Like a telegram with bad news, these few words arouse all the hours of bad feeling that long arguments used to achieve in their youth. When a couple has had the same quarrel 1400 million times, they can follow it without effort like a train follows a railroad track. Many elderly couples sit side by side in wheel chairs, and if they don't have the strength to hit each other they need only say one code word to be able to reminisce and have all previous bad feelings without having to carry out the quarrel. They still have their memories and imagination, even if they hardly have the strength to argue. Therefore, one should not consider old age a desert but look forward to it as a time when one can have an awful marriage even if one has only the strength for minimal moves. People in old age also still have something to look forward to. Many of them believe they will be with their relatives in the afterlife to come. They can glow with the anticipation of continuing unfinished quarrels, and having new ones, in the place beyond time.

THERAPY—A NEW PHENOMENON

Among the mysteries of human life, there are three special ones. What is the nature of schizophrenia? What is hypnosis? What is the nature of therapy? These mysteries share aspects in common. All of them involve paradoxical communication in a way that is exasperating to the theoretician who would like, as Gregory Bateson would say, to get them "to lie flat on the paper." All of them are controversial; each has groups arguing over its definition and nature. In each case there is a question raised whether it even exists.

Of these mysteries, therapy has become the most important issue. Vast sums of money are involved in the art and science of changing great numbers of people. In the scientific field and in the marketplace enthusiasts contend about the many different kinds of therapy. I will discuss here, rather informally, my own adventures in the years I have taught and done research on this topic. I have been led to a certain way of thinking about, and doing, therapy which came partly from my teachers, especially Milton H. Erickson, and also from research. The research influences, which I will emphasize here, led me to uncertainties and confusion about this phenomenon over the years and finally to a logical position about therapy.

I began my research life in the 1950s inquiring into, among other things, the nature of schizophrenia, hypnosis and therapy. In that decade all three phenomena underwent a basic change from being individual to being considered interpersonal in nature. Schizophrenia, for the first time since the word was coined, was thought of as a behavioral response to a social situation. Families and hospital staffs were defined as part of the malady, leading to therapeutic milieus and family therapy. Hypnosis, which had always been considered a one person phenomenon, began to be defined as responsive behavior to another person. Instead of being the effect of magnets, or a relaxation or sleep phenomenon, hypnosis was examined as a peculiar response to the peculiar behavior of a hypnotist. The work of Milton H. Erickson with his emphasis on the interpersonal induction of trance had its influence in that decade. Erickson also had his influence on therapy which for the first time began to be thought of as an interpersonal phenomenon in the 1950's. Prior to that time one could read the literature of therapy and not find what a therapist did in an interview, because he, or she, was really not there. The focus was on the patient and his hopes, dreams, past, and projections upon the therapist. In that decade it was discovered that what a patient said was a response to what the therapist was doing, not merely a report on his inner nature. As Bateson said, a message is both a report and a command, and so involves more than one person. I believe the first published interview of a therapy session, not just an anecdotal excerpt, was by John Rosen in 1948. He had mimeographed interviews and he also printed a verbatim therapy interview with a patient diagnosed schizophrenic. To read the dialogue of two people talking in therapy, and not just a case summary, was a revelation about both schizophrenia and therapy.

It is curious that in the decade of the 1950s everyone began to think more socially. Animals were studied in their natural environment by ethologists, the organization of businesses became a focus, and all kinds of groups became popular. Families were actually observed in action and for the first time the behavior of a therapist became part of the description of therapy as audio and visual recordings were used. Cybernetics, the science of self corrective systems, provided a theoretical framework for the group processes being examined.

As an aside, a major influence on those of us who were viewing therapy as interpersonal was Harry Stack Sullivan. I was supervised by Don D. Jackson who had been personally supervised by Sullivan. To illustrate the change in thinking at that time, I was doing therapy with a hospitalized patient diagnosed schizophrenic and had been seeing him daily for a number of years. One day this gentleman began an interview with me by saying something like, "I was out on my submarine this morning, and we were to meet the refueling ship off Madagascar, but unfortunately the ship had been struck by an atomic bomb and barely limped in late with its Chinese flagons at half mast." The routine therapeutic response would have been based on the idea that the patient, since he was locked up in a hospital and did not own a submarine, was expressing the fantasy of a disordered mind. The question might be whether he was speaking randomly or expressing a symbolic meaning based on childhood experiences. Because of Sullivan's influence on Jackson, I had to face the question how the patient's comment was related to *me*. I realized that I had been late to the interview that morning. The talk of a refueling ship being late could best be received as a courtesy comment on my lateness. By courtesy, I mean it offered me the opportunity to interpret to him what submarines really symbolized to him, or to apologize for being late. Those were the days when schizophrenics were the great teachers in psychiatry, before it became the fashion to drug them.

Does Therapy Exist?

As we look at these great mysteries today, it is the nature of therapy that has become the most explosive in the production of theories and innovations. It is also the most difficult to research. When we research a topic we prefer a well defined field where we can gather facts and make hypotheses. Studying therapy, we would like to know what the facts are, what theories explain them, and what techniques are most successful in inducing changes that are well defined. When I began research on therapy, just what and how to investigate it was not clear. In fact, the question being asked seriously for the first time was whether therapy actually existed in the sense that it was causing a change. Was there a correlation between a therapist's behavior and a desired change in the client, or was therapy an illusion? The fact that it was practiced by prominent people and had been done over several generations did not necessarily mean that it was not illusory.

There have been a number of scientific endeavors which proved to be delusions. We might remind ourselves of the science of phrenology, the study of character by the shape of the skull and the bumps on the head. That science was thought to be based on facts and had many enthusiasts among scientists in universities. There were national and international journals reporting research findings for many years. We have dismissed it as an illusion today, but it is a lesson for us all that many intelligent people can be misled for long periods of time.

Can we say that today there is much more evidence for the existence of therapy than there was in the 1950s? The number of clinicians has increased by the thousands, and the number of schools of therapy has multiplied. Yet there does not seem to be increased certainty about therapeutic theory and practice. We still face the unsettling question of whether therapists influence anyone at all.

When I began research in the 1950s, outcome research on therapy was beginning to indicate that therapy was not causing a change. Equally interesting was the investigation of spontaneous remission. One form this investigation took was resarch on the changes which occur when a client is on a waiting list anticipating therapy in the future. The findings were that from 40% to 60% of people on a waiting list recovered from their symptoms. Because of our observation of families at that time, it seemed possible that spontaneous change could actually be greater than that. The merits of waiting list research were debated, but it was extremely important whether a high percentage of people recovered from the problem without therapy. It would mean that when a person happened to be in therapy at the time of spontaneous change, the therapy would get the credit. Assuming half of any therapist's clients recovered if the therapist just kept out of the way, the therapist who did nothing would be the most successful in achieving his 50% cure rate. Therefore therapists would be encouraged to do nothing as a sound therapeutic approach. With half their patients getting better they would feel rather confident about their therapy approach. Believing therapy is bringing about the change, the therapist would live in a financially stable illusion. It was not only the examination of waiting lists but the discovery of families and how they change that led to uncertainty about the effect of therapy. Let me cite a case, as one should when talking about therapy, to illustrate the difficulty in defining what is a problem as well as the issue of spontaneous change.

A 19-year-old woman was referred to me for a shaking right hand. It was an uncontrollable, intermittent shaking that had persisted through a year of therapy and a number of negative neurological tests. She was referred to me to cure the symptom with hypnosis while her psychiatrist continued to work on the roots of the symptom in her childhood, which was a curious arrangement I sometimes made at that time. I asked the young woman what would happen if her symptom became worse. She said she would lose her job because she was having increasing difficulty even holding a pencil to write. I asked what would happen if she lost her job. She said her husband would have to go to work. This helped me to think of the symptom as interpersonal, which I was trying to do at that time. I learned she had been married recently, and her husband was unable to decide whether to go to school or go to work. Meanwhile she was supporting him. The symptom could be viewed as a marital issue. Yet discussing her marriage, I found the issue could be defined as a larger unit. Her parents had opposed the marriage and continued to do so, not approving of the young man. Each day her mother would telephone her and ask if she was coming home that day. She would point out to her mother that she was married and had her own apartment now. Her mother would say, "That won't last." Mother continued to call, encouraging the young woman to give up her husband and return home. It seemed to me the shaking right hand and the husband's behavior could not be explained without a family view. The husband seemed to feel that he could not please his wife's parents whatever he did. If he went to work, it would be a job not good enough for their daughter. If he went to school, they would object that she was working to put him through school. So he was incapacitated.

I made a variety of skillful therapeutic interventions in this case, and the outcome was successful. The shaking hand was cured, the husband went to work, and the parents began to support the marriage. However, in my period of self congratulation I could not overlook another change which had occurred during the therapy. The young woman became pregnant. Once pregnant, she was going to have to quit her job, and so her husband went to work to support her. Her parents, who wanted her back home, did not want her home with a baby. They began to support the marriage. The symptom disappeared. Since she was in therapy at that time, the therapy got the credit, and I got more referrals. Yet I think the change she went through might well have occurred if she had been on a waiting list.

This case, and others, helped me to give up the view that symptoms are deeply rooted in the individual, and to consider them adaptive to a social system. They can come and go as the life situation of a person changes. Naturally, the longer people are in therapy the more chance there will be of a positive change occurring in their lives independent of the therapeutic action.

It is not only possible that therapy has little effect, but equally possible that the confidence of the therapist in his theories will not be affected by the outcome. We would like to believe not only that we can determine what is therapy and what is not, but when it is effective and when it is not. Our certainty that we are causing a therapeutic change is often taken as evidence that we are doing so. When I began to investigate therapy, I became acquainted with some unsettling research which made me cautious about having confidence in theories. Alex Bavelas, a social psychologist, was a consultant for me on an experimental program into the nature of normal and abnormal families. In his own research, he was investigating the ways human beings construct theories. I will summarize a particular experiment which I don't believe he ever published.

In that experiment, Dr Bavelas gave subjects a panel with many buttons and a light. He told them the experiment was a timed test. Their task was to find out which buttons to push to make the light go on. The subjects would begin to push buttons and watch the light. After awhile they would be able to make the light go on by pushing the right series of buttons. They would explain, for example, that it was necessary to push the button in the top corner, then the one in the lower corner, then the one in the middle twice, and then the third one from the end, for the light to go on. They could demonstrate the proof of their theories by pushing the buttons and making the light go on again and again.

When they completed their task, Dr. Bavelas might or might not tell the subjects that in fact the light went on every 20 seconds no matter what buttons they pushed. They were living in an illusion that their acts precipitated an event which, in fact, was occurring independently of anything they did. Just as the therapist can have the illusion he causes a change in therapy when it is actually the result of other actions, so did these subjects live in an illusion. Some of the subjects refused to believe it when they were told they were not turning the light on. The higher they were in academic status and scientific background, the more sure they were that they were turning on the light by pushing the right buttons. (Some of them would only give up the delusion when they put someone else through the experiment.) After that, I listened to clients and families with a more cautious concern about finding patterns.

In my research on therapy, I tried to examine whether we were inducing changes as we thought. The fact that several generations of therapists had believed in the theories and the results did not mean the evidence was sound. Let me cite another experiment by Alex Bavelas which might portray the history of therapy. In this theory building experiment, Dr. Bavelas would tell his subjects that he wished them to develop a theory in an area where they had no knowledge. He would show them, for example, pictures of cells, and he would say that some of these cells were sick cells and some were healthy cells. The task was to look at the cells and guess which were which. Since the subjects knew nothing about sick or healthy cells, they could only guess. Dr. Bavelas said he would tell them if they guessed correctly.

Now in actuality the cells shown on the slides were randomly selected; none were particularly sick or healthy. In addition, Dr. Bavelas was following a program. He told the subjects they were correct 60% of the time no matter what the subject said. That is, when they guessed whether it was a sick or healthy cell, 60% of the time they were told they were correct in their guesses, and 40% of the time they were told they were wrong. The reinforcement was not contingent upon what they said; it was independent of their responses.

The subjects would look at a cell and make a guess, then look at another cell and make a guess, and they would begin to build a theory. They would decide that a sick cell had a little shady area, and a healthy cell did not. Since they were told they were correct only 60% of the time, they would soon find that they were wrong when they said a cell with a shady area was sick. Therefore they would decide something more was needed. They would add the idea that there needed to be a shady area and a thing hanging down, and that was a sick cell. Again, they would prove to be wrong since they were told they were right only 60% of the time. As they studied the cells, they had to increase the complexity of their theories of what is a healthy cell and what is a sick one.

When the experiment was completed, Dr. Bavelas would ask each subject to write down his theory of the difference between sick and healthy cells. He would offer a new subject this written explanation and tell him that the previous subject had worked out this theory on the basis of his guesses. The new subject was instructed to take this theory, use it if he wished and correct it if necessary. The new subject would examine the theory and look at the slides. He too was told he was correct in only 60% of his guesses, and so he would find the theory he had been given was only correct about half the time. Therefore he would have to add his own complications as he made his guesses. In doing so, he created a more complex theory which he was asked to write down and pass to a new subject, a third generation. This new subject would examine the theory and do the same task. The third generation subject would look at this more complex theoretical description and begin to apply it to his task of guessing sick or healthy cells. He too was rewarded as correct only 60% of the time. Naturally, he found the theory was not quite adequate, and he would add to it and make it even more complex.

When Dr. Bavelas approached the fourth subject and gave him the same instructions, the subject would look at the extraordinarily complex theory, say, "The hell with it," and discard the theory. Starting over, he would make his own guesses and build his own more simple theory based on being correct 60% of the time. After constructing his theory, he would be asked to write it down and pass it to the next generation of subjects, and so on.

Dr. Bavelas found a sine curve. Theories would become increasingly complex over the generations until a revolution occurred and previous theories would be discarded. Subjects would start over again to build increasing complexity over the generations until someone discarded the theory again. I think this might be a description of the history of therapy, if not of all scientific endeavors. If we accept the idea that every therapist will have a 50% to 60% good outcome rate when doing therapy, independent of the action in the therapy, he will make a hypothesis about how his therapy works which will increase in complexity as failures occur. He will pass it on to the next generation who will find that it is correct about 60% of the time and will add complexities to the theory to improve it. They will pass it on to the next generation. At a certain point, young therapists will say, "Let's start over and think this business through in a new way." They will make a more simple theory, and so on.

I think it might be argued that behavior therapy began as a rejection of the theories of psychoanalysis which had become increasingly turgid and so complex they were hardly understandable. Now behavior therapy is becoming increasingly complex with intricate learning and cognition theories. Similarly, many of us began family therapy as an attempt to make a simpler theory and discard past complexities which were not relevant to the therapy task. At this point in family therapy we have enthusiasts who are creating more turgid and complex theories with their circular, epistemological adventures.

In summary, we face the possibility that our theories of therapy are based upon processes of spontaneous change and not upon our actions. If so, we will have a reasonably good outcome, a high level of confidence that we know we are producing change, and the consensus of colleagues and teachers. As the number of generations continue, we will believe theories are improving when in actuality they are only increasing in complexity to account for failures. All of this can happen without the outcome of our therapy being contingent upon our therapeutic interventions. That is the framework of uncertainty I faced when teaching and doing research into the nature and practice of therapy. It is still the situation today.

What is Therapy?

Besides wondering whether therapy actually has an influence, those of us doing research need to determine what is therapy and what is not. Just as it is difficult to say what is schizophrenia and what is not, or what is hypnosis and what is not, therapy is difficult to separate out from other activities. Is good advice therapy? Is accidental, random influence that has a positive effect therapy? If a violent person is hospitalized and medicated, is that therapy? If so what of the criminal placed for rehabilitation in the penitentiary?

We might define therapy as a client voluntarily seeking a therapist in order to change, yet that is only one context since therapists work with involuntary clients both in and out of institutions. We cannot examine therapy without examining its social context, and what is new in the world is the use of therapy to restrain people. Responding to public disorder, the government provided funds for mental health centers in poor neighborhoods and a therapist there had to deal with the question whether he, or she, was an agent of social control or a therapist helping a client. There are other questions about whose agent the therapist is. Is the therapist the agent of the state? In a family, is the therapist the agent of parents who want a child restrained? In a marriage, is the therapist who sees a wife for her anxiety the agent of a husband who would like to pay someone else to listen to his wife complain?

In the last few decades we have seen the social impact of therapy developing everywhere in communities, and we can no longer think of therapy as simply the interchange between two people. It is a business, a calling, and the agent of many forces.

Is Therapy the Same Everywhere?

At one time we could do research on therapy with the assumption that therapy was relatively independent of its context. However, today therapy is done in so many different ways in so many different places that such simplicity is not possible. Obviously, the practice of therapy is going to be different in different contexts: therefore the theory appropriate to it will change with the context. For example, a therapist in private practice who has wealthy clients, or insurance which pays for the therapy, will have a certain theory and practice. In that situation a therapist does long and leisurely therapy exploring the nature and origins of the client's discontent. The theory appropriate for that context would allow the uncovering of subtle ideas in the person's psyche, anticipating the slow overcoming of resistance, and assuming that there is a long history of past influences which determine present thinking.

Such a theory and approach would seem bizarre in a mental health agency dealing with the poor and working class. Faced with a drunken husband, an erring wife, and a delinquent son, none of whom want to be in therapy but are required by the court to come, how can the leisurely exploration of childhood fantasies be considered? In such a situation, a therapist must develop a theory that current influences are a consideration in therapy, that redistributing power in a hierarchy and organization is important, and that rapid change can be brought about by action and not reflection. The goal must be a behavioral change rather than a shift in the content of a fantasy.

To researchers these two extremes indicate that therapy must change its nature when it changes its context. In relation to the financial context alone, the private practice therapist paid by the hour and the agency therapist on salary are going to develop different theories about the pace and depth of therapy. To quote that great theoretician Mark twain, "Tell me where a man gets his cornpone and I'll tell you what his opinions are."

It is possible that the most important decision in the history of therapy was the idea that it should be paid for by the hour. Suppose, in contrast, that a therapist was paid a set amount for successful outcome with a problem. Would theory and practice not change? We might see that day as insurance companies, who determine so much about the nature of therapy, consider orienting themselves to brief contracts for specially defined problems successfully solved.

Who Should Do Therapy?

In the period of time that I have studied therapy, not only has the nature of it come into question but inevitably who is to do it and how are they to be trained has changed. As therapists began to unionize by getting licensed, they had to argue that their training was of such a nature that they had the right to tamper with people's lives and other people without their training should not. Yet there is the curious problem that all the professions require different training. If psychiatrists agree that psychologists should do therapy, they admit their years of medical training are irrelevant. If psychologists say that psychiatrists or social workers should do therapy, they are saying their years of testing and research are irrelevant. If social workers say that psychiatrists and psychologists can do therapy, they are saying their courses in the history of social work are not essential to a therapist. While this issue was being debated in the established professions, there was an eruption of new people entering the field through family therapy and various forms of counseling who were outside the established professions. If they were allowed to do therapy, all that the professions had been teaching was not necessary.

I began to do therapy without proper training, whatever that might be, and I once trained others who were not even college educated to do therapy. They were quite competent in doing therapy even though they lacked not only graduate degrees but also what all middle class therapists had experienced, an undergraduate education. In the 1960s the poor came into therapy. We either had to teach the middle class therapist to understand the poor, or we had to teach the poor to be therapists. We did both. Setting out to train people from the community to do therapy, we discovered that much considered essential to be a therapist was really not necessary. The degree, the education in philosophy and psychology, the courses on testing, all seemed not essential when people off the streets could be trained to be competent therapists if properly taught and supervised. Obviously, whatever therapy is, therapists can be trained in many different ways and still do as well, perhaps even better, than waiting lists.

The Use of Metaphor

Besides all the social issues which arose during this period, a theoretical problem existed from the beginning of therapy investigations. The theoretical analogies, or metaphors, trapped everyone into a particular way of thinking and so helped prevent us from conceptualizing the new forms of therapy developing. It would seem to be in the nature of a theory that it can restrict thinking. In this particular situation the analogies were too limited to deal with the complexities and changes in the field.

I recall a learned and prominent psychoanalyst beginning a lecture by saying, "We all know what is strength and what is weakness. A muscle is strong, or it is weak. It is the same with the ego. The ego is strong or it is weak." This kind of analogy was typical of the time. In actuality, the ego is a hypothetical entity, an abstraction created in an attempt to explain some behavioral phenomenon. To consider it strong or weak like a muscle and set out to strengthen it, presumably with therapeutic aerobics, is to take a metaphor literally in a most curious way. Interestingly, in all three areas of mystery there is a confusion about the literal and the metaphoric. In schizophrenia, the person often says things like, "I have butterflies in my stomach when I get nervous, and they are blue and yellow." In hypnosis, metaphoric images are accepted as literal, as part of the nature of trance. In therapy, we use analogies, stories and metaphors to influence clients who respond to them as to a literal message. Or, we create a metaphor as part of theory building and take it literally.

When I began research, not only was the ego taken literally but the entire intrapsychic structure was so real inside a person that it was as if it could be examined with a surgical operation. There was also the confining analogy of the steam boiler. It was said that if a conflict did not burst out here from internal pressures, it would burst out there in a symptom. It might be noted that a much more sensible analogy for people in relation to the steam engine was the idea of the "governor" which controlled it, proposed by Maxwell in the 1870s. That did not become adopted as important until the cybernetic theoreticians made use of it almost a century later in their theory of systems.

There was another analogy, or metaphor, which handicapped us all and is still a source of confusion. Used to build theory, it also was used as a polemic against competing theories. It was suggested, as part of an old tradition, that the important entities for therapy within the human being were vertically spaced. That is, the conscious was up at the top, and the unconscious was down below. With that analogy one could speak of bringing something "up" into consciousness or putting something "down" into the unconscious. It was also possible to give "deep" interpretations because one knew that the important area was "down there" in the roots, not up here in the superficial surface. One could, as a polemic, say that the other person's therapy was "shallow" while one's own therapy was "deep." That was often said about those of us who did brief therapy by people who did endless therapy and called it deep.

I wonder how many hours of seminars and controversies have been devoted to that up and down metaphor? One can appreciate how limited it is by considering other alternatives. Suppose it had been agreed that the unconscious was to the left, not down below, and the conscious was to the right? One could say, "My therapy is more leftist than yours." One could also say, "I made a far right interpretation." An objection to brief therapy could be that it was "rightest" rather than shallow, with a whole new set of connotations.

A research difficulty for years was finding ways to measure a "deep" change in therapy in contrast to a "shallow" change. Now we can see that the most serious problem in research is to escape from such analogies and recognize when we attempt to describe change that we are talking about real people doing things in the real world.

How Many Theories are Necessary?

Once it was thought that a single theoretical structure could include all aspects of the clinical field: it could cover diagnosis, research and therapy. It was not thought necessary to have one theory for research and another for therapy, or one theory to explain etiology and another theory to describe change.

Psychodynamic theory is an example: it had categories of diagnosis, it would create testable hypotheses for research, and it would encompass interventions for therapeutic change. Similarly, learning theory would provide all the framework necessary if one took that approach in the clinical field. Family therapists assumed that systems theory encompassed everything and could explain etiology as well as change.

As we look at the field of human relations today and see how it has been necessary to bend and stretch theories to make them all encompassing, it seems possible that different theories are necessary for different purposes. The etiological theories of psychodynamics do not lead to a set of therapeutic operations. For example, a person might be an extremist in collecting shoes so that he has closets full of them. He could be diagnosed as compulsive, and the origin of the problem would be found to be fixations in childhood. Similarly, a person afraid to go out on the street would be called a phobic and the fear traced to past traumas or hidden wishes. Yet the theory does not lead to a set of operations for reducing the number of shoes in the closet. Nor does it describe how to have the phobic person take steps outside. The most one can do with that theory is to continue to explore with the client the etiology of the problem and hope it goes away. It does not follow from the theory that there are 7 strategies for bringing about change in the shoe collection acts. Those procedures would follow from learning theory, but learning theory would not have as interesting and seductive an idea why the person collects shoes. The psychodynamic theory also cannot include thinking about how to involve a husband in the therapy of an agoraphobic wife so that the wife can go out as far as both spouses can tolerate.

Usually the theory of why people are the way they are is the most seductive and interesting theory, and so clinical students get involved in that view rather than a theory of change. In academia it is difficult to teach actual therapy operations. The theories of how people became as they are usually is what is taught.

It seems more evident in family systems theory that the theory of the cause of a problem does not help when one sets out to make a change. The idea that people are caught up in sequences and keep repeating certain behavior because of self corrective processes operating is an interesting one. One can see, for example, that improvement in a child can lead to a threat of marital separation which leads to a relapse of the child followed by the parents pulling back together. That is an excellent theory for explaining stability. But how is it for a theory of change? It not only does not lead to obvious interventions for change, but it is an anti-change theory. When thinking about changing a system, it is better to think in a linear, hierarchical way and therapeutic operations become evident.

It is interesting that the issue of free will has come up in a new form with systems theory. If one assumes that a person does what he does because of what someone else does, which is the view of systems theory, then there is no individual choice. Yet it is a question whether therapy could be done with such a deterministic view: therapy assumes that a person must be thought of as responsible for their acts. A theory explaining why something is done is not necessarily helpful when seeking to change the situation.

As an example, one can explain wife abuse as a systemic phenomenon: the wife provokes the husband who hits her, and then the sequence repeats itself. The cooperation of the two people is a way of explaining why the abuse happens. Yet if one is setting out to stop the violence, that theory of their mutual contribution is not a useful one. A linear intervention is necessary.

One might also add another theory as necessary in the field. If one is setting out to raise normal children, the clinical theories are not helpful. It does not seem reasonable to allow a child to do anything so he will become unrepressed, as in psychodynamic theory. Nor does it seem reasonable to have the parents firmly in charge in a hierarchical way, as one might with a structural intervention with a problem child. What is done when something is wrong is not necessarily appropriate at all for what is to be done in normal living.

In summary, the field of therapy now has the complication that a theory is necessary for diagnosis, another theory for aetiology, another theory for therapeutic change operations, and another theory for describing normal living.

Guidelines

Let me review some of our uncertainties about therapy and their relevance to current practice. We cannot be sure that therapy actually influences people, and the fact that previous generations were sure does not make it so. When we examine therapy, assuming it exists, we have trouble saying what it is and what it is not. Not only is it difficult to differentiate from social control activities and educational processes, but it seems obviously to differ in different social contexts. It is not a single type of behavior. When we try to think about therapy, we are confined and restricted by clinical metaphors and theories not relevant for change. Given all these uncertainties and doubts, how can a responsible therapist and teacher act today? How should we proceed if we are not to delude the public paying for our services? To a great extent it is these uncertainties from observation and research which have led me to the particular kind of therapy I developed and teach. There are certain guidelines for a therapy which seemed to me to be the most trustworthy. Let me outline them.

1. If it is possible that change occurs independent of therapy, with a risk that the therapist is taking the credit when he should not, it follows logically that therapy should be brief. If clients are seen for years, they graduate from school, get married, have children, get divorced, and go through all kinds of life's changes which can, in error be attributed to therapy. Short term interventions can better reveal whether it is the therapy or outside forces which are inducing change.

2. When there is uncertainty about change, it would seem better to focus upon the most observable situation and not dwell upon what cannot be seen. It follows logically that one should be concerned with the current, real life situation of a client, which can be examined, rather than the past for which there is no evidence, or fantasies for which there can be none.

If one wishes to believe that a person's past will program his, or her, present it becomes part of the goal of therapy to change the past. With skillful reframing techniques that we use today, and with the careful use of amnesia, it is possible to keep people from having the awful pasts they once had. The use of amnesia is particularly valuable. It seems that we can get along with each other if we forget today what we did to each other yesterday. To reframe the past with psychodynamic ideology and so bring out all its worst traumatic aspects seems less helpful than to reframe it in a more positive way and give amnesia for the worse of it.

3. If there is uncertainty about how to verify the outcome of therapy, it would seem logical for therapists to focus on a particular problem. In that way one can determine whether the problem is still there or not. To accept for therapy ambiguous character problems or system relationship problems when one can never determine if they were successfully changed does not seem reasonable.

4. To gather evidence about what is happening in the life of a client, as well as to determine if therapy is inducing a change, it would seem best to bring in the family. Not only can the family contribution make therapy more successful, since relatives inspire changes that a therapist alone cannot, but it helps the therapist stay in the real world where change can be observed. A wife who offers only fantasies about her husband is not providing the information that arrives when she provides her husband. What a handicap it now seems for therapists in the old days to have declined to see relatives or even to speak to them on the telephone because it would interfere with the therapist's fantasies about the family.

5. If one wants to be more certain whether the therapist has an influence or not, it seems sensible for the therapist to focus on behavior and give directives for change instead of only talking about ideas. To discuss issues insightfully leads only to a change in the client's ability to discuss insightfully. A behavioral change can be observed. This issue is separate from the fact that people are more cooperative and less resistant to change if one does not make interpretations or give insight.

6. If one wishes to influence a client to change, it logically follows that a therapist should organize the therapy so that happens. To sit back and listen and say "Tell me more about that" is to produce a therapy without destination. If therapy is to achieve a goal, the therapist must set one. To get there, the therapist must, as much as possible, arrange what happens as much as possible. It seems naive to let a client initiate all con-

versation, behavior, and ideas when the client has come because he does not know how to change.

7. If we wish to be sure that we are not taking money under false pretenses and our therapy is changing someone, it would seem logical to train therapists in skillful therapy techniques. Just as therapy should focus on the observable present, training should focus upon the observable actions of a therapist, preferably on videotape or in a one-way mirror room. To depend upon personal therapy of the therapist as a way of teaching how to change a client is to avoid training a therapist how to change anyone at all.

Perhaps most important, it is reasonable to wish a therapist to have confidence in his, or her, ideas and actions in therapy. The past emphasis on personal therapy produced therapists who were uneasy about their unconscious conflicts and hostile, aggressive, internal impulses. It now seems naive to teach therapists self distrust and then expect them to confidently offer hope and help to the helpless and unfortunate.

These guidelines are based upon a rather obvious idea about therapy, and what becomes evident is a curious finding. It seems apparent that the procedures I am recommending for therapy are precisely the opposite of what was done 30 years ago when I began my therapy investigations. At that time, and still occasionally in the large cities, there were some assumptions: it was assumed that therapy should be long term, it should deal with the past and not the present, it should not focus upon a problem but upon vague character issues, all relatives of a client were avoided, insight and interpretation were the therapeutic focus instead of action, a person was helped to remember every miserable moment of the past, and training consisted only of personal therapy for the therapist.

There was another issue which shows a difference from the present focus of therapy: in those days a therapist did not take responsibility for change. If someone asked an analyst "Is it your job to change people?" the analyst would say it was not. The task was to help people understand themselves; whether they changed or not was up to them. The opposite posture seems more reasonable today in terms of accountability. The therapist is no longer a consultant but a people changer who fails if the case fails. As Erickson would put it, a therapist must learn many different ways to change many different kinds of people, or take up some other profession.

In summary, the kind of therapy we have today as the mainstream is the opposite of what was done in the past. Some people have changed because of the influence of teachers, others out of trial and error, and others after examining therapy research. Today there is a generation of people who have seriously taken up the career of changing people. They are not advisors or consultants or objective observers or diagnosticians. They are people whose task it is to be expert at influencing another person. They are skilled at getting people to follow their suggestions, including suggestions the person is not aware that he, or she, is receiving.

We have arrived at a revolutionary time in the therapy field. Rather than being pessimistic about whether therapists influence people at all, as I suggested was the beginning of therapy, we are now concerned that therapists will become so skillful at influencing people that we must worry about how to govern therapists.

Although therapists are not extraordinarily skillful today, let us project into the future and see what it might be like if present trends continue. There will be a group of skillful people who have spent years of training and practice influencing people. They will know how to give directives that are followed and know how to influence people outside their awareness. They will be able to marshal the forces in the family and the community to bring about the changes they wish. Groups of such therapists will combine their thinking in planning strategies to produce change. With therapists and their teachers becoming increasingly skillful in their craft, therapists will use power over other people to benefit them. What about limits on that power?

When we look at the three mysteries of human life, people have always been afraid of schizophrenia and they have been afraid of hypnosis. The time is approaching when therapy could raise fears and in fact, already has. As we train therapists to be experts at influencing people, their skills must be confined to positive goals. It is a problem that teachers in the martial arts faced when they taught the most scientific ways to use physical force in combat. It is not helpful to say that therapists should not be interested in power, when skill in achieving power over others is often necessary in helping people. It also does not seem reasonable to teach therapists to be inept as a way of preventing their influence. Obviously we want therapists who can help people in distress because they are skillful and know their business. But how will we control these people who are becoming expert at controlling others?

Logically it follows that training therapists in technical skills must be within a framework of ethics and self discipline. Our problem becomes more complicated as so many different kinds of therapists enter the field, and as therapy becomes more of a business and less of a calling. Technical skills can be used to turn people into patients for financial gain as well as to change them. Possibly the model to turn to is one developed by others who needed to control people trained in the skillful use of strength and power. We might ultimately adopt a model from the martial arts and Eastern religion where people are taught ways to achieve power within a framework of harmony and restraint. An adaptation of the Aikido philosophy is appropriate. We could form a society and define therapy as: "The art of defending oneself and society without taking advantage of, or harming, other people."